Standing Room Only

STANDING ROOM ONLY

THE ENTREPRENEUR'S GUIDE

JASON BARBERA
AND RICK HEAGARTY

ISBNs: 978-0-9993619-0-0 (paperback); 978-0-9993619-1-7 (ePub); 978-0-9993619-2-4 (Kindle)

Library of Congress Catalog Number: 2017913445
Printed in the United States of America
First Printing: 2017
20 20 19 18 17   5 4 3 2 1

Takedown Publishing
360 Quecreek Circle
Smyrna, TN 37167

Cover design and book design by Ryan Scheife, Mayfly Design and typeset in the MillerText and Adoquin typefaces

This book is dedicated to Krissy

—Rick

*to my wife, Aoibheann who is the center of my life
and my wonderful children Lochlann and Dempsey-Rose.*

to my parents and family for always loving and supporting me

—Jay

Contents

Standing Room Only

X pro is all about innovation—it says so on our company's website. But there's more to that than meets the eye. Much more.

We'd like you to innovate how you approach your business—and your life, for that matter. And it starts with building an environment that's Standing Room Only.

We're Jay Barbera and Rick Heagarty. We're the principal owners of Xpro Supply and Xpro Commercial, a building material distribution company located in Nashville, Tennessee. Our differentiator—what truly sets us apart—is that we provide installation services for every product we sell at every level of a project—both commercial and residential construction. Serving the southeastern United States, we offer a broad range of services from the beginning of a project to final wrap-up.

Our slogan, "Where Innovation Gets Built," tends to grab your attention when you arrive at our website's home page. From a practical standpoint, that's completely true. Whether in the heart of renovating a multi-family structure or overseeing a new residential development, our material distribution company prioritizes innovation at every level, from pricing to addressing customers' particular needs to ensuring that each and every project is completed on time and within budget. Given the spotty quality that many consumers have to tolerate with all sorts of products and services, we firmly believe our ongoing commitment to those sorts of high standards is innovative in and of itself.

But, for Xpro, innovation means a good deal more than that. The principles upon which we built the company—principles that we adhere to every day—are, in their own way, every bit as innovative as the Xpro projects that dot the southeast. It's an approach to business—and life—that's simple and straightforward, but one that is often overlooked, ignored, or made needlessly complicated.

If you operate a business—or merely dream of owning one—we challenge you to read our story, hear our ideas, and, from there, make both your business and your life all that they can be.

The Meaning of the Standing Room Only Message

Most everyone understands the term "standing room only." It means an event where every seat is taken to the point that people are standing wherever there is space available. But it's not just logistics. It represents something worthwhile and valuable—something people are happy to attend, no matter if they have to stand the entire time. The experience is more than worth it.

Rick's Story: My Mom's Memorial Service

I don't mean to start our story with a morbid anecdote but, in reality, the example I'm about to share is anything but purely sad or depressing. My mom died prematurely. But, before she did, she wrote out exactly how she wanted her memorial service to be conducted. She was literally lying in bed and I listened as she wrote out and instructed our family exactly who was to say what and when. It was kind of surreal.

But what was even more amazing was the event itself. Her memorial service was so well attended that it was, in fact, standing room only. The local police were outside directing traffic because there was such an overflow of people and cars. It was standing room only, both inside and out.

The point about standing room only is that you often never really understand or appreciate how many people's lives you touch with your own. That was one of the many wonderful things I took away from my mom's service—and an element that lives to this day in the way we do business at Xpro.

When we first started the company, we both wrote down three things that we wanted to achieve. Amazingly enough, of the three, the only item we had in common was a desire to touch people's lives, to make them better. We feel we've done that and, through this book, we hope to touch yours as well. That's the principle and strength of standing room only—an inclusive approach that lets you know how many lives you've influenced for the better. That's the real meaning of success.

Rick, Jay, and Xpro: The Path to Today

Whether brick and mortar or virtual, bookstore shelves are teeming with books that detail all sorts of business success stories. In that sense, Xpro's is no different. From 2012, our first full year in business, we have grown at a rate that is almost unbelievable. We expect that growth to continue.

In many ways, though, the Xpro story takes a very different path—one we feel can be replicated by others looking for a business that's successful, personally rewarding, and offers a healthy balance between professional responsibility and personal life.

Start with timelines. Conventional thinking holds that it takes most businesses several years just to break even, after which come years of modest growth.

To which we reply: bullshit. (By the way, that's another thing you'll notice about this book that's different. When something is bullshit, that's the language we use to point it out. It's straightforward, to the point, and not open to interpretation. It gets the message across.)

The reason we label that conventional timeframe bullshit is that there are alternate ways to come up with different ideas to jumpstart a business, to really springboard it. We want to challenge people to question that assumption. We'll get into specific nuts and bolts later on.

Our ideas don't necessarily run counter to the principles taught in business schools. We simply don't limit them to numbers and abstract concepts on a page. The academic approach gives you strategy, marketing concepts, and financial ideas. What they're not telling you is how to knock on a door and sit down with somebody and make them feel comfortable enough to give you money, or to give you business, or to want to continue to give you business. We believe in education, but it's not necessarily the most important thing. It's relationships.

We've grown our business quickly and efficiently. A lot of that has to do with the intangibles that we bring to every customer relationship. We have an enormous amount of positive energy. People like to be around us, they want to be social with us, they want to laugh with us—and oh, by the way, we've got a great service we provide at a very fair price.

Nor has our remarkable growth come by way of an "any job, any time, anywhere" mentality. In our early years of the company's development, one of us had to dissuade the other from taking on particular projects—not because they weren't lucrative, but because they weren't "right." And that boiled down to the relationship with the customer and where that could go and where it could not.

Relationships aren't limited to customers happily scratching checks for a job well done. For us, success also mandates responsibility to all of our employees that make our business work.

That translates to commitment, whether it's encouraging personal, everyday initiative on every employee's part or company-wide meetings every six months where the rule of thumb is absolute candor in speaking your mind on whatever topic you think important to the company's future. There, we make it abundantly clear: tell us what we need to hear, not what we want to hear.

And it works. Oddly enough, about a month or two after those meetings, we see a huge spike in sales. That really matters to all of us. While we as the leaders are the ones who have our asses on the line, we're also the ones who are taking care of our families.

If all this seems just a tad different from other business books, that's not an accident. If you haven't already, take a quick glance at the table of contents. Some topics will undoubtedly engage you, some may surprise you. Some, frankly, may offend you.

But that's perfectly OK by us. No matter the topic, we'll always keep your attention, and that's what matters most.

What also matters is the Xpro story, the lessons it affords businesspeople and entrepreneurs of all sorts, and the overriding importance of a sense of balance: a commitment to providing top-tier service, a determination to achieve financial success but never once losing sight of the relationships that make everything come together—again, the standing room only principle.

What makes all this work is relationships with customers, relationships with employees, relationships with your business partner, and relationships with your family. That's the secret. Many business owners reverse a formula we know to be true: as owners we work for our employees, customers, and families, not the other way around.

You'll see what we mean over the course of this book.

Things here are standing room only, but we always have room for one more. Glad you could join us!

Chapter Two

Open Kimono

You're thinking about starting a business. Or maybe you already have one.

In either case, you're giving some thought to bringing on a partner or partners—starting from the moment you open your doors or adding one or more to an established business. Maybe you had a partner before who didn't work out and you're thinking about giving someone else a try.

No matter where you happen to be in your business life or the reasons you're giving a partner some consideration, be ready to open the kimono. It can be the tipping point between a business that truly takes off and one that continually struggles to achieve all that it truly can.

We know that from firsthand experience. Our partnership has been one completely built on an open kimono. And that has made all the difference.

Open Kimono Defined

You may have heard the term open kimono before. If you haven't, it simply means complete transparency. You are hiding absolutely nothing. An open kimono represents complete candor, all the time.

An open kimono has proved critical to our success, be it with customers, employees, or anyone with whom we work or have a relationship. In this chapter, we'll discuss how it applies to choosing and working with a business partner.

You may already have a business partner or, by the same token, may have never considered taking on a partner. Our ideas about the open kimono will still prove valuable to you. Maybe you can make an existing partnership work better or, if a prior partnership went south, maybe a new one can turn out far better. Maybe—just maybe—our discussion will convince you that a partnership is not the way for you to go.

See what we did just there? In laying out the value of this chapter, we did it with an open kimono—straightforward, forthright, no confusion. We sincerely believe this discussion will be beneficial to anyone reading this book. That shows the value of the open kimono, no matter the circumstances.

Rick's Story: Young Man, You Need a Porsche!

When I was a young man and was just about to graduate from college, I was doing the job interview circuit in a big way. I was talking with every company that came to campus, either for the practice or a job opportunity. In particular, a large financial company seemed to be interviewing everyone in sight, including me. As part of the interview, they administered a handwriting analysis and a Myers-Briggs test (the well-known test that evaluates psychological preferences and identifies how people make decisions). As it happened, I did well enough on all counts for them to invite me to their offices for a second interview.

Well into the conversation, the partner who was interviewing me looked me in the eye and—without even a trace of sarcasm—said, "Rick, you need to go out right now and lease a Porsche." My first thought was, "This guy is absolutely crazy!" Since I was in a job interview, I managed to express my surprise in a more dignified manner and asked him what he meant.

"Based on your personality profile and your handwriting analysis, you're the kind of guy who will go out and do whatever it takes to make that Porsche payment and not compromise your integrity or your company's integrity," he explained. "I'm offering you a job right now, right here today, and I want you to go out and lease a Porsche."

The practical side of me repeated: what is wrong with this guy? There I was, in the early 90s, no job, rent due, and this guy wants me to add an extra $1,000 in lease payments?

But, the more I thought about it, the more the whole thing seemed less crazy all the time. For one thing, the guy was being absolutely forthright with me. Based on what he saw, he had confidence in my ability to succeed and was willing to use a challenging measuring stick—a Porsche payment—to show me just how confident he felt.

Open kimono, all the way.

But, in terms of our discussion about choosing a business partner, the experience also raised the question: how do you find someone who's not only going to meet all you may require in a partner but is also going to be perfectly comfortable in a relationship that's completely open kimono—one who's not going to bat an eye when it comes to being completely transparent?

The Open Kimono Partnership Checklist

With the value of hindsight, we've drawn up a series of questions that we feel can be valuable in vetting a potential partner—and, in effect, ensuring an open kimono relationship. The first question is one only you can address:

1. **Why do I need a business partner?** This may seem an obvious question but it's often overlooked or downplayed. Maybe you've got a buddy you'd like to work with or just feel that two heads may be better than one. Those aren't the worst reasons in the world, but it's important to give serious, detailed thought as to why a partner might make sense. Don't be afraid to dig deep—and, in the spirit of open kimono, don't be shy about telling any prospective partner precisely what you're looking for. Some possibilities to kick start your thinking:

    a. I'm a Type A personality who needs a Type B around. For instance, if you're an action kind of person, would someone more thoughtful offer some balance? (That's been the case with our partnership.)

    b. I don't have certain skills—organizational, financial, what have you—that someone else can supply.

    c. I need the capital. Maybe you have marketplace skills—loads of contacts, great sense of the market—but need someone with the financial resources to get things moving. We'll address this more specifically later in this chapter.

2. **What's your potential partner's financial situation?** This is an important question no matter the circumstances, but especially so if one reason for a partnership is necessary capital. If a potential partner is financially secure and tells you that he can live off $35,000 a year to get things rolling, that may hint at someone who's ready to do whatever's necessary to drive the business' success. On the other hand, if a guy

has three ex-wives and alimony payments from here until Sunday, that may not be a lasting solution if you need reliable finances. Regardless of your needs, a partner's financial stability is always a plus.

3. **What's your potential partner's personal situation?** Is there something in your potential partner's family life that could derail the partnership down the line? Is there an ex-spouse who excels at being a nonstop pain in the ass? Is there an elderly parent they take care of? These are all issues you need to know up front before you make any sort of decision—an open kimono discussion. That's not to say we would say no to someone in that situation. We'd just want to know about it because that's an obligation that's likely not going to change. Again, open kimono.

4. **What is the potential partner's standing in the community?** This means a lot, no matter if you live in a small town or a large metro area. Do you want a partner people respect and enjoy seeing, or someone who's always looking over his shoulder because he hasn't treated others well? It's essential that you and anyone connected with your business fit into your community. You don't want a partner who doesn't show up for his kid's Little League games because he might run into someone who's suing him. The same holds true in the industry in which you work. Does a potential partner go to industry functions because he enjoys seeing his peers, or does he stay away from them like the plague because most people think he's a shmuck? Whether good or bad, a partner's standing among other members of any community you're a part of is bound to impact your business sooner or later.

5. **Does he see your value proposition?** Everyone
   says they offer great service, great prices, and great
   after-the-sale support. Everyone says they're the most
   professional people in their field. That doesn't separate you from your competitors in the least. Your
   value proposition is the most unique differentiator
   you have—it's essential that your partner understand
   it. It can't be interchangeable with everyone else's. In
   our case, our differentiator as a company is we provide
   turnkey services for all of the material that we sell.
   That means a builder doesn't have to go out and chase
   down labor and supplies. That means less time on the
   job site and less time in the office managing invoices.
   Just as important, it sets us apart from others who
   don't offer that comprehensive level of service. It's
   essential that a partner understand your value proposition and be able to convey it.

6. **What's his commitment to the business?** Ask if your
   would-be partner stays until the job is done or is out
   the door at 5 p.m. no matter what. Ask about an example when he went above and beyond to ensure success.
   No matter if it's a coffee house or an architectural firm,
   your level of commitment should be the same. Anything short of that can lead to resentment and a toxic
   work environment.

7. **How does he define success and failure?** For some,
   success means making a half million dollars a year.
   For others, it's a successful business that lets them
   spend plenty of time with their family. For us, success
   means much more than the cash in your bank account.
   That's not to say financial success isn't great—it is—but
   there's more to success than dollars and cents, at least

to us. As we mentioned in Chapter One, there's the importance of relationships with family and friends. The same holds true for failure. For some, failure begins and ends with financials. For us, failure means not letting our families down, however that can happen. No matter how you define success and failure, it's valuable that any partner be in step with you. Differing views of success can eventually clash.

8. **How does he define a business' culture? What sort of culture is he interested in?** These are also telling questions, in part because the word "culture" means so many different things to different people. For one thing, some don't think a company's culture is all that important. We couldn't disagree more—in our case, company culture has everything to do with our success. If you were to meet us all individually, you might think we were some of the oddest people you ever met (picture the Island of Lost Boys from *Peter Pan*) but, collectively, we are a strong, cohesive unit because there's something unique about each and every one of us. We're different, but also like minded in that we're all working toward a common goal and supporting each other as we do so.

Since we know firsthand that culture is powerful, it's important to gauge how a prospective partner views it. Is it the energy you show in the workplace? Is it the vibe when you walk through the door? Is it how people dress when they come to work? Whatever it might be, it needs to be consistent and it needs to be embraced.

You just can't downplay culture.

9. **What would he do if he didn't have to work?** This is a really important issue to us. It shows what someone truly values and would be involved in if making a living were out of the picture. Would they just sit on the coach all day and zone out on reruns of *The Price Is Right*? Do little more than try to bring down their golf handicap? Or maybe something a bit more substantial, such as starting a business that helps young people or fledgling entrepreneurs? How about volunteer work or some form of philanthropy? If it's something they don't have to do yet they pursue it with commitment and enthusiasm, that speaks volumes about their character and personal priorities.

10. **What's the exit plan?** It may seem weird, but this may be the most important question of all in terms of the open kimono. Partnering in business is great, but let's not kid ourselves—nothing lasts forever. That said, how does your prospective partner plan to leave? What would he do if things simply didn't pan out? What if they did work out and you're looking at shifting ownership—either passing it along to a family member or selling it outright? Knowing how you'd like things to end can make the journey toward that goal a lot more transparent—and, likely, successful.

Obviously, there are many more questions you can ask—feel free to do so. For instance, ask them to describe a time they were in a tough situation—maybe they'd run out of cash temporarily. How did they handle it? Did they dip into their savings? That can show how committed someone may be to a business—even one that's teetering on potential disaster.

It can also be helpful to have the other person define what the ideal partnership means to him. Does that suggest absolute equality or does one of the partners have the final say? How will the partnership involve others in the decision-making process?

What we're saying is, use this list as a jumping-off point. When chatting with a possible partner, take the conversation in the direction that's most effective. Of course, encourage your prospective partner to ask questions as well, as they can also be very revealing about his values and what he might bring to the partnership. Be as open kimono in your answers as you wanted him to be.

Also, have the conversation in a setting that works best for you. For some businesses, coat and tie in a boardroom might be consistent with company functions and values. By the same token, beer and barbecue at the local rib joint can help break down inhibitions, provided it doesn't run absolutely counter to your business and its culture. Go with what's comfortable and, at the same time, the best setting to bring out the best possible dialogue.

Lastly, don't overlook any essential paperwork and agreements that are central to an effective partnership. These include buy/sell agreements, non-compete agreements, confidentiality statements, and key man life insurance. A partnership can be impacted or fall apart for any number of reasons, so be certain that your interests are adequately protected. Defer to your lawyer's expertise so nothing is overlooked.

Share the Kimono

Our partnership has been central to the growth and success of our business. But, it's important to point out that we have a third partner, one whose contribution to the business differs somewhat from the synergy we two have but is no less central to our success. Mike Morgan is the managing partner and CEO of Xpro Supply. (How he came to work with us is laid out in Chapter Twelve.) Mike also holds an equity share in the company.

That last item might send some people's heads spinning. For

many, giving up an ownership share in a new business runs counter to everything they've been taught. Never, ever dilute your financial ownership.

To which we reply: it's made all the difference in the fast growth we're so proud of. Here's why.

First, we got out of the blocks that much faster. Given that Mike had an established presence in the local construction community, we immediately picked up customers and market share. Had we gone that alone, we would have likely struggled to find a foothold. With Mike, that was already in place.

Additionally, the results were evident in our financials. Bringing Mike on board gave him an equity position in the business but, at the same time, our sales exploded in our very first month of doing business.

So much for that bullshit about having to wait three to five years to break even!

Just as important, that sort of financial kick-start allowed us the opportunity to really work on our business—our procedures, philosophy, and other elements that have also boosted our success far faster than conventional wisdom might suggest. That's a competitive, internally built advantage, one that many start-ups out hustling for every sale they can find can't even imagine.

In choosing to work with Mike, we employed the same guidelines of the open kimono that we've used in every aspect of our business. We were completely forthright, as was he. And, thanks to his varied contributions, insight, and experience, our business has been able to grow much faster—and been that much more fun as well.

The Value of Open Kimono—With or Without a Partner

In the end, you may find a partner who's ideal in every way. You may find one who meets most of what you're looking for. Or, quite possibly, you may decide that a partnership doesn't really meet your needs—at least now.

But, by following the principle of the open kimono, you've locked onto a strategy that's going to be of enormous benefit to you and your business in all sorts of ways—whether that's in your relationships with your customers or suppliers or in your hiring of and relationships with your employees (which we will cover in the next chapter). No matter who's involved, complete transparency is the key to a successful business that's built on great relationships.

It's All in the Culture

We've never hired a successful employee by using a want ad. We tried it once—just once—and the hire quickly fizzled.

That provided us with an important lesson, one we want to make sure we pass along up front. Now that you've established an open kimono relationship with your business partner as well as any other business relationships, it's time to apply that idea to the other people who will make up your business: your employees. And that starts with looking for and identifying people who understand and embrace your culture.

We talked a fair amount about culture in the prior chapter. Culture is critical when looking for the best employees for your business. Maybe that's why our attempt at using an ad to hire employees fell flat. It was too open ended. It said, in so many words: "We need someone. Who's interested?"

Our system of hiring employees begins from a very different starting point. In a way, we already know when we're talking with someone about coming to work for us that they're likely a good fit. They're not there just because they picked up the phone or used an email to respond to an ad. They're there for a much more valuable, meaningful reason—one that helps ensure their success with us for years to come.

Culture—Largely Unspoken, but There

As we said, culture is everything when hiring the best employees you can find. What's ours like? Here are a few key points:

- We're professional at all times, but we value fun.

- We have confidence in our employees to make intelligent choices.

- We've never told people when they have to be at work or when they have to leave.

- We've never told people what they have to wear to work.

- We've never told people what they have to say at work.

- We empower all of our people to run their own division.

Those and other aspects of our company may not seem earth shattering in terms of being unique, but they have worked extremely well for us. That's because we hire people who we know embrace those values. As we said, we don't have a clothing policy, but we can't remember the last time someone showed up to work naked.

That also means we don't spend a lot of time developing policies and procedures. Granted, those are important, because you have to have some sort of line in the sand. But we like to think of those as moving lines, ones that can be flexible because, again, we have the right people in place to begin with. With the best employees, you just don't need a whole bunch of rules. And that starts with culture. If you try to hire without knowing your culture, you're going to be like a sheep wandering around a pasture. You'll be lost.

Nor, in our hiring process, do we spend time throwing our culture into people's faces. We don't like doing that, nor do we need to. That's because, as you'll see, by the time we get to the point of talking with someone seriously about working for us, we already have a pretty good idea of how they'll fit into our culture—and, just as important, that they understand our culture and embrace it.

The Process of Hiring the Ideal Employee

Want ads just don't work for us, so we never use them. So, how do we identify potential employees?

For that, we rely on our network of business associates, friends, and other people whose opinions we value. We talk to everyone we can think of. If possible, we start by getting to know prospects socially. Our people are hand-picked based on our culture and the background we pull together from people throughout the community and in the market in which we do business.

If you think this can take a lot of time, you're right on the mark. It can literally take months for us to hire someone for a single position, particularly managers. For one thing, many of the people whom we hire aren't looking for a new job when we approach them. A contact may say, "Hey, if you guys are looking for someone, there's a guy I know who would be a perfect fit." That sort of thing.

That's also because we vet them so thoroughly in advance. In fact, we generally interview only one person for each position. By the time we hire them, three to six months may have passed from when we began the search, but we understand that's the process that works best for us. It's helped us gain the success we've earned over a short period of time.

The actual interview can be very much off the cuff. We don't script them because, since we've done so much advance legwork prior to meeting with an applicant, each situation is likely to require a different set of questions.

In many ways, the interview is very subjective. How does this person feel to us? How does he respond when we ask about his values and his approach to work? But we also look for subjective, subtle things. If someone is going to be meeting with customers, does he smile a lot during the interview? Those and other subtle hints tell us whether people will mesh with our culture.

Since we know our culture, we know what we're looking for. People who learn rapidly. People who understand strategy and our market. People who have a broad knowledge about our business, who understand teamwork, have a sense of humor, and understand our value statement. We look for people who will work in the best interest of our company without it being explained to them word for word.

What we don't ask are a lot of the stereotypical questions you associate with job interviews. For instance, we won't ask where someone wants to be in three to five years. If you run a good company and are committed to helping someone grow, you already know the answer! They'll still be with you, contributing just as you expected them to contribute.

We do ask about their comfort level when it comes to risk. That's not so much to do with risk itself but their confidence level. If someone says they're comfortable with risk, they're likely going to be comfortable and confident when they walk into a sales meeting with a total stranger.

(As an aside, we've heard most every sort of answer when we've asked about risk in a job interview. We once asked someone what his biggest risk was. Buying a house, he replied. Another time, an applicant said his biggest risk was a very explicit sexual encounter that he videotaped and posted on YouTube. That's the range we're talking about—one whose biggest "risk" was something everybody does and another who needed to be diplomatically escorted out of the building.)

Generally, we don't worry too much about how a person looks. Granted, if someone comes to interview and his belly is hanging over his belt, that's two strikes from the get go. As we said in the prior chapter, our staff resembles the Lost Boys from *Peter Pan*. That's an accurate description. Personal appearances aside, how a person looks matters less than what they bring to the company and how they embrace our culture.

But looks can matter on occasion. We had an employee we wanted to promote. We loved everything about the guy—we'd identified him straight off to be a leader in the company—but we did not like the way he looked. He had an earring and tattoos everywhere. Not the sort of impression we wanted to convey to customers or, for that matter, employees.

That just didn't fit with a leadership role, and we told him so. We said he had to change his appearance, take out the earring and cover up the tattoos. He came back the next day. The earring was gone, he was wearing a shirt with a collar, hair combed, professional as they come. We promoted him on the spot and it's worked out beautifully.

That's an important example in several ways. First off, it was an open kimono approach. We knew the way he looked when we first met just wasn't going to work, and we said so. And, once he had changed his appearance, there was no sense of his having compromised himself in any way. He knew what our culture required and he accepted that. Again, the importance of culture helped us pick the absolute right candidate for the job.

The Report Card—in the Interview and on the Job

In many ways, our hiring process is very subjective: look for people who buy into our culture and pay attention to our gut feeling when talking with them. To a certain extent, the same holds true for employee management: not a lot of rules. If we hire the right people, we have confidence in them to do the right thing.

But it's not completely subjective. When hiring and, after that, evaluating employees, we use a carefully thought out grading system to gauge if someone is a good fit and, from there, how they grow into their role in our company.

It's a simple system, like a letter grade in school. It's A through C, along with a plus or minus.

Let's start with the A people. These are the employees we really rely on. They're the ones we delegate to, who give us peace of mind when we go on vacation. They're not afraid of losing their jobs and they take thoughtful risks. They want to move up. They understand our value proposition and care if the company doesn't do well.

Bearing that in mind, there are very few A people. Nor is there such a thing as an A employee—at least over the long term. The best grade we've ever given an employee is an A minus. Why? If someone moves into A status and stays there—or even moves up to an A plus—it's time for them to move on. They're going to keep bumping up against you and they're going to push you to the point you may not want to be pushed.

The majority of applicants and workforce are Bs. These are the people you want. You work with them to develop them further, maybe pushing them toward an A minus. Or maybe they're a B minus and you're trying to push them to a B.

Bs can be your very best applicants. First, they may be more affordable than an A applicant. Culturally, they're more likely to stay with you longer as they look to further develop themselves. That makes Bs the mainstay of your workforce—often as much as 80 percent.

Lastly, there are Cs. You never hire a C. They may be lacking in certain skills you require or, by the same token, don't buy into your culture. Moreover, if someone you've hired begins to fall into C status and stays there, it may be time to gently begin working them out of the company.

A few things about our grading system. First, it's entirely private, known only to ourselves and individual employees. Also, we sit down and review every employee's grade every three or four months. We go through how an employee is doing and evaluate where they've made improvements and where they need to do a better job. That means many employees can "float" between various grades.

Although we try to be as flexible as we can, we generally don't wait too long if an employee's performance and grade continually struggle. For one thing, we always have a Plan B in place with our employees—what we need to do to work together to help someone who's having a hard time improving. We always give that person an opportunity to correct himself, but we don't let him go it alone. We will always sit with him, review in detail those mistakes he's making and what we can do to help him better his performance.

We try to be fair, but we don't allow too much time to go by. As a general rule, if someone's still making the same mistakes thirty days after we started to review them in an effort to improve, we'll start giving some thought to letting him go. It's not fair to the company, other employees who are performing well, or the employee himself to keep him around longer than his performance warrants.

It's also a question of attitude. For example, we let one guy go who kept repeating the same mistakes but didn't display any willingness or desire to change. He was taking advantage of us and we knew it. It was an inherent form of behavior that we knew wouldn't change. Like they say, a leopard never changes his spots. Those spots can fade sometimes, but they're always still going to be there.

Nor is our involvement always the best solution to an employee who's experiencing problems. When we first hired one of our supervisors, he could never make a decision. He must have called us five or six times a day, asking what he should do. It was crazy!

We knew he had to take ownership of his division and responsibilities. The answer: We made a conscious effort not to return a single email or phone call from him. Not one. We completely avoided him for three weeks.

He was freaking out! He thought he was getting fired! Finally, we spoke to him and asked him if he had made any decisions during those three weeks. Of course, he replied. And did he cause any irreparable damage to the company? No. He quickly gained confidence in his decision making.

At times, to best help an employee improve at his job, you've just got to be willing to remove the training wheels without their knowing it. It's like teaching your kid how to ride a bike. At some point, you take your hand off the back of their seat, but they think your hand's still there. And they finally look back when they crash in the grass and realize you're fifty yards behind them. Inevitably, they say, "Oh, shit. I can do this."

Choosing the right employees and doing whatever's necessary to help them excel—and, sometimes, that may be absolutely nothing—not only boosts the overall performance of your company, but it can also have enormous personal rewards. To that end, here's an email we once received from an employee who had been struggling with certain aspects of his job. He sent it late at night, likely after a few hours of soul searching:

> "Hey, guys. I just wanted to thank you for the great opportunity you've given me to help build and grow with the company. I appreciate your trust in me and that you stand behind me, even when I screw up. I know we're going through a rough spot right now and I'll take the blame. I'm in charge of my staff and it's up to me to correct it. I know I'm not an owner, but to me this is my company as well as yours. Sorry to ramble. Thanks, guys, for everything."

Hiring from the Gut Versus the Heart

When we emphasize how subjective our hiring process is as we look for people we believe will embrace our culture, don't take that as an overemphasis on emotion. That's because what few mistakes we've made in our hires were the result of decisions that came from the heart—not our guts.

Happily, we've had only a few. We hired one because he was the son of a friend. Big mistake. We cut him loose very quickly. The second was a guy whose wife worked here. It was Christmas and he needed the job, so we thought we were doing the right thing by hiring him. Right it may have been from an emotional standpoint, but it was a pure sympathy hire. He lasted only three days.

Another was the son of a friend. The kid had just graduated from college and, as we knew the father very well, we thought he would be ideal. Not so. We let him go within a month—although, we're happy to say that we still maintain a relationship with his dad.

Finally, there's a really interesting example. We once hired a guy who was able to keep up when we were a small business. But, when things really took off—when the small business went to medium and then to a large business—the operation outgrew him. We had to let him go. Our explanation was that the company was moving faster than he could keep up—a concept to bear in mind when you're looking to hire new people. They may seem an ideal fit now, but what happens in a couple of years when the business is more demanding and moves faster?

All this raises an important point, especially for someone going into business for the first time. If you're going to be a business owner, understand up front that you are going to have to fire people as well as hire them. If you are naïve enough to think you're never going to have to fire anyone, you're crazy. Accept it. It's no one's idea of a great time, but know that you'll have to let people go, so you need to be prepared to do it in a straightforward, dignified way— once again, the open kimono.

The Importance of a Reset

To restate: we generally take a hands-off approach to employee management. Hire the right people, and things usually take care of themselves from there.

But hands-off only goes so far. Over the years, we've learned the value of periodically resetting and tightening things up. So, coordinated with a review of an employee's grade, we have a reset exercise. That means bringing everyone in individually and going through a brief refresher—not only covering how their performance has trended of late, but also chatting about our values, culture, and any other topic that we think is pertinent.

Complacency is a weird thing. We all tend to fall into patterns of habit, both for the good as well as the bad. On the downside, that can result in simply going through the motions, carrying out your responsibilities without giving any thought as to what's really effective and what could stand a change in perspective or approach.

We also use these "reset" sessions to get past the pitfalls of short-term memory. If it's the height of the building season, often all we hear are people saying how busy they are, how overloaded their calendars are, and how there simply isn't enough time in the day to accomplish everything. That may be true but, in our reset sessions, it never hurts to remind our people of how slow things might have been in the heart of winter and how much time they had on their hands.

Overall, the reset lends perspective while planting the seed of balance. When things are crazy, slow down and take things as they come. When things are quiet, use that time to your advantage to plan for when things inevitably pick up. And, when things start to ramp up, that's when dealing with customers in the most effective manner possible becomes our top priority. That's the focus of the next chapter.

Chapter Four

Checkmate

This chapter has an attention-grabbing title, particularly for those who play chess. That's intentional, because it's as important and valuable as any other portion of the book.

The concept of checkmate is a tipping point for many businesses. To be blunt, it's where many businesses fail.

No matter what business you happen to be in, we don't want to let that happen to you. So, let's get started by examining how you can outmaneuver, outperform, and, ultimately, checkmate every possible competitor you may run up against.

Action Versus Static

Think about the issues we've covered to this point: partnerships, and hiring and managing employees, among others. Those responsibilities can all be handled by most anyone. For instance, is there any great trick to writing out a business strategy? Not really.

Most people who operate a business have a business plan. That may be a common practice, but we believe most business plans—as they're written—are pretty much one small step above worthless. That's because, once a business plan is in place, many assume that everything's going to go according to that plan—all nice and neat, end of story. The truth is, we all know that almost nothing goes according to plan. There's the mistake that many businesses make: putting absolute faith in something that doesn't warrant it.

The difference boils down to being static versus taking action. A business plan is naturally static, but it isn't worth a thing if you can't execute it properly—and, as needed, adjust it to adapt to shifting market conditions. We have a saying: your strategy should be written in pencil, but your execution plan should be written with a Sharpie. A pencil can be dull and fuzzy when you use it. A Sharpie is bold, distinct, and permanent. There's the difference between planning and action. Most people can write out a strategy. Very few know how to execute it.

First, Ask Some Questions

Before you can begin carrying out your plan to get to checkmate—in other words, putting your strategy into action—it's essential to ask a few critical questions. Here are a few to get you started:

- What's your core competency? By that, we mean what's your company's sweet spot, strike zone, or your true wheelhouse? Don't just say we sell tires, prepare taxes, or repair small engines. Dig deeper to pinpoint your true core—for instance, you specialize in high-performance tires and accessories or you focus on tax planning for small businesses and the self-employed.

- From there, ask yourself what you're really trying to do. Are you trying to be customer-centric, or are you trying to highlight the products that you offer? Maybe you're truly aiming to be operationally excellent. This takes the idea of identifying your discipline and really puts a face on it.

- What's your differentiator? What makes you genuinely different from others in your field? What sets you apart from everyone else? It could be as simple as the way you bring things to market or the way you prospect for customers. It could be the way you deliver your materials or services. This is not what the market necessarily feels makes you different, it's what *you* feel is different—the idea that you can grab onto, take to market, and say, "Here's what sets us apart."

- What's your market equation? What's your opportunity? What's your volume, your capacity to take your product or services to market and excel? In other words, what can you reasonably do and what simply isn't reasonable (at least for now)?

You can see what we're getting at here. Anybody can determine who their likely target might be. It's also a matter of the plan to go get them. So, once you answer those questions, what's your strategy to execute your plan? And what's your dashboard to monitor your results? This takes the static side of the equation—planning—and pushes it into thoughtful action.

Rick's Story: Fast Freddie

My dad is a natural teacher, a coach, and he was the best man in my wedding. So needless to say, I owe him a great deal based on the leader I have become today. My dad did a great job of showing me how to connect information and experience with actionable results.

I'm reminded a great deal of the lessons he shared with me in my childhood that I use to this very day. First, like many businesses that draw up a strategy, you think it's all going to go according to plan. Everyone's going to stay on the boat or in the nest. But, many businesses that draw up a plan realize very quickly their plan for execution is worthless and, for that matter, self-destructive.

What I learned is that, when mapping out a strategy to bring a plan to execution, you need to *think* quickly and clearly because you're going to need to *act* quickly and clearly. As we'll discuss later in the chapter, you're going to need to adapt. If you move too slowly, writing out some lengthy plan that doesn't take execution into account—execution that occurs quickly and clearly—it means you're busy writing while your competition is out taking your business. Without an execution plan, you lose in the strategy phase, and nothing else from there really matters.

First Steps

Like every great chess player, strategy translates into an action phase—taking the static planning that most every business draws up and putting it into motion. Let's discuss why we chose these terms to describe the execution of business strategy.

Your first moves are critical. By that, we mean you move forward without prejudice and do whatever is necessary to make contact with the people you need to reach, be it through broad networking or pounding the pavement and knocking on doors. Believe us, we aren't the biggest fans of this stage—there are lots of other things we would rather be doing. But it's essential.

Also, no ninja shit here. When you make your first moves, you want people to see and hear you coming. No guerilla warfare, no black ops bullshit. This is World War II and you should hear our tanks coming from two miles away.

The reason is simple but overlooked. It's critical to be visible in the market. You want a high presence. You want to generate buzz. You want people to talk about you, to know you as a very trustworthy, honorable organization. When that's your message, you don't want to do anything quietly. You want people to hear you coming because you've got nothing to hide. The last thing you want is to be under the radar.

Next comes the moves that precede ultimate victory. That means taking everything of value. Leave nothing on the table. If our customer says he wants a roof, windows, siding, and doors, we're going to give him all of those things. We're not going to say no, we'll just give you gutters. Make sure you do the same with your business, whatever it might be. If the customer wants it and you can provide it, don't ever come up short.

Lastly, checkmate. If you've done the first two steps, checkmate happens automatically. If you've generated buzz and connected with customers who will come back and do business with you over and over, there's the burn. There's nothing left behind for your competitors.

Measuring Your Campaign

This overall strategy can propel your business to levels of success faster than you can imagine. But it's important to have a measuring stick—a gauge of determining whether your efforts and execution are, in fact, successful.

That can come in any number of ways, both simple and sophisticated. For instance, setting a goal of increasing revenue by a certain percentage over a certain amount of time is a perfectly adequate way of measuring success. Maybe it's the number of new clients, new jobs, or some other growing level of activity. However you choose to do it, don't make the assumption that your efforts don't need to be measured to accurately underscore and interpret their success. Many businesses that struggle fail to do this or fail to do it consistently or in a meaningful manner—another example of an inability to execute.

Here's an example of what we're talking about. Recently, our guys in the warehouse were high-fiving over a two-hundred-delivery month. They were going crazy! That was great, but what did that mean? Looking at it more closely, we tried to calculate how many deliveries was the optimal number per job. Our operations manager agreed that three deliveries was a fair amount of deliveries. That led to the question of how many they were making per job—how did those two hundred deliveries break out? I don't know, the manager answered, maybe five or six.

We then pointed out that, even though the number of deliveries we were handling meant we were really busy—and that was great— we needed to be aware that, the more deliveries we made to a particular job, the lower our profit margin per load. So what did two hundred deliveries really mean? Did it mean a high level of profitable activity, or could we be more efficient and profitable with just 150 deliveries to the same number of jobs?

That's what we mean by having a meaningful measure of success. It doesn't blind you with misleading statistics—in this case, a lower number of deliveries was actually a positive. That means we needed to carefully examine what the idea of success really meant— and, from there, taking steps to execute more effectively.

Execute, but Be Flexible

Our calculation of the optimal number of deliveries per job raises another key element in a successful campaign: flexibility. Many businesses that draw up a business plan and, from there, execute, tend to see the plan as carved in rock—since someone spent a lot of time and energy drawing it up, it should stay as it is, no matter what.

That's another major mistake. As we discussed earlier, few things go the way you expect or plan for. However confident you may be in your strategy, it's critical to be flexible—to change your thinking and your execution as market conditions and other factors dictate.

Here's another quick story to illustrate that. In the early days of the company, we came up with this great idea involving "buckets." We drew up a big list of customers we were going to go after. But how were we going to get them? We each knew them in different ways—professionally and socially. There were also some product lines that some of us were familiar with and some weren't.

We ended up creating buckets that held different kinds of customers that we would approach in different ways. We honed it further by adding margins and volume and started putting customers in those buckets based on the type of builder that they were. That allowed us to target buckets for cash flow to run the company on a day-to-day basis, and other buckets that might not be as active but offered really high margins. Our thinking was balance. It was far better to have ten customers accounting for 10 percent of our income versus just one customer tied to 90 percent of what we were earning. It was a really slick system.

It worked really well for us but, as we learned over time, nothing bats a thousand indefinitely. Although we still use our system of buckets, we're constantly adjusting our allocation percentages. It has a great deal to do with shifting market conditions and changing customer lists. For instance, we've found that, the more we sell to particular customers, the longer they tend to stay because of the way they've integrated with our company. That, in turn, can prompt an adjustment in the percentages between various buckets, balancing cash flow and high-margin projects.

It's not a completely perfect system. We work on it all the time, trying to find the ideal mix. It's nearly impossible to set something up for a year and just roll with it. You might be able to get away with setting a three-month timeframe. But the time comes when you're looking to change again.

But, in a way, there really is no perfect system—rather, there's a commitment to execution, flexibility, and balance. And our bucket allocation strategy let us achieve all three of those elements, provided we stay on top of it—another example of a commitment to execution, not just strategy.

Example: Checkmate—from Planning to Execution

To help you grasp the nuts and bolts of our checkmate system, here's a real-life example that we used when mapping and executing a plan for projects in the Nashville, Tennessee, metro area:

Strategy

We began by calculating our market equation. In other words, what was our market opportunity? We knew that Nashville had five thousand projected new home starts for one year in our service area. Based on our customer profile, we figured that 25 percent of those new starts would fit in our target market. That percentage derived from the price range of houses—$300,000 to $650,000—that matched the products we could offer builders with projects within those cost parameters.

From there, we further honed our market opportunity based on how much siding, roofing, decking, windows, gutters, exterior accessories, and cabinets were used on an average home in that price range:

- Average cabinet price-: $15,000

- Average siding: $4,000

- Average roofing: $3,500

- Average decking: $1,500

- Average windows: $3,100

- Average gutters: $1,100

- Average exterior accessories: $1,500

- Total average: $29,700

Next, we injected a dose of reality. Since the $29,700 figure was based on selling all components, we estimated selling roughly half that amount on average. That brought down the average to $14,850.

From there, it was just a matter of a little math to calculate the total market opportunity: five thousand starts divided by 25 percent—our projected share of the overall market—multiplied by $14,850. Our market opportunity was approximately $18 million.

Execution

Next, what would be our execution strategy to move into that $18 million opportunity? We did our research and built a big list of builders who matched our price band. From there—using our "bucket" methodology again—we profiled each builder by evaluating the types of products they used in their homes.

Further, we wanted builders who valued product domination and customer intimacy. Product-domination builders were easy to pinpoint because they promote and market the products they use, either in print or model homes. Since it's a behavior, connection with customers was more difficult to identify. We interviewed, scrubbed, and fired several prospects to find those we considered a match for our services. (We'll cover this process in greater detail in a later chapter.)

Once we had a target list in hand, we moved. We "attacked" with individual meetings in which we spent our time selling our value proposition and differentiator. In this particular case, our differentiator began with a very simple phrase: "F**k up less."

That started as an internal joke, but we massaged it into an appealing message. When a potential customer would ask us, "Why should I do business with you?" the answer was simple: "Because you'll have more time to spend with your family."

At first, this would elicit a look of shock, almost bewilderment. But, remember, we targeted builders who valued personal relationships. That meant their relationship with us as well as their loved ones. So, it was a simple but powerful form of execution. The customer would provide a set of plans, we'd provide a material list, the customer would purchase their products, we would deliver and install and assign a project manager to oversee, and provide ongoing advice and guidance—all on time and within the authorized budget. That eliminated several job site trips, needless subcontractor phone calls, management meetings, and expensive administration time.

The result: Less "F**k up" and more time spent with family. It worked like a charm.

This example is obviously geared to the building industry, but it's a strategy that can be applied with most any business profession. It's strategy, but a strategy borne out by thoughtful, actionable execution—the difference between businesses that continually struggle and those that successfully checkmate their opponents, time and again.

Chapter Five

Make Your Customers Count

Anyone who's thinking about starting a business may be tempted to give the subject of customers relatively little thought—at least in terms of numbers.

What's to think about? Grab hold of as many customers as you can. Keep the checks rolling in.

That's understandable, but just a little too simple. If you want your business to take off from the outset and continue on an upward trend over the long haul, it's vital to know what kind of customer you want to attract and work with—and, once you have them, how to feed and take care of them.

Make Them Count

In the early days of a business' lifespan, everybody wants to forge ahead and take every job they can get, no matter what. They're hungry for volume, plain and simple. Say no to no one. The customer's always right. Customer strategy? We'll figure it out as we go.

That's certainly easy to see. You're just starting out and assume that you simply can't afford to be picky in the least. But, even if you've got a line of customers coming in through the front door—volume, volume, and more volume—you'll learn over time that some of those customers can tap into (and drain) your resources more than you might have bargained for. That's why you need a well-defined strategy to identify those customers who will truly serve your best interests—those who will remain with you and help you grow.

Put another way, it's important to make your customers count.

What We Look For (and You Can, Too)

We have some pretty basic rules in our company so far as the sort of customer we are interested in. First up are personal issues. We want people to be respected. We don't want any of our people mistreated in any way, because we never do that ourselves. That doesn't mean we're looking for mirror images of ourselves. Granted, it would be nice if our customers were just like us in terms of personality—in fact, we're pleasantly surprised when we do come across someone like that—but it's more a matter of having confidence in their ability to understand us as much as we try to understand them.

That also doesn't mean we avoid working with a customer who has a different personality. What it does mean is we all know what boundaries are in place from the very start of our relationship.

In fact, we're open to adapting our style to make customers feel comfortable with us. We listen, communicate, and work to figure out what makes a guy's wheels turn. Not only is that flexible and good business sense, but it's also realistic—at the end of the day, if there's any discomfort in the relationship, we don't want to be the ones who are uncomfortable, since we were the ones who were willing to adjust. It's going to be the other guy who's going to be uncomfortable.

"Buy the f**king cabinets, you p***y!"

Here's an example—a colorful one, if you like—of our adaptability in working with customers. We had a prospect who was working with one of our top people about buying cabinets. As it happened, we also knew this prospect very, very well—we knew what the customer was comfortable with and what might set him on edge.

At one point, I asked how things were going. "Okay," replied our rep, shrugging. "We've got him on the fence, but I'm not really sure if he's going to move forward or not."

What else could we do? I grabbed my cell phone and immediately hammered out a text message: "Buy the f**king cabinets, you p***y!"

Business 101, right? Well, what did the guy do? He bought the cabinets, of course.

Granted, that may not be in every business' playbook, but it illustrates how we come to know our customers and understand what they'll respond to. In this case, I knew the customer wouldn't be offended. Instead, he'd get a laugh out of it and appreciate the "forwardness." It also demonstrates, as we'll get into more detail about later in this chapter, that we make a point of listening to our customers—not just wining and dining them, but really learning what makes them laugh, pisses them off, and, ultimately, gets their attention.

Also, we weigh the overall value of each customer. By that, we mean we're not focused so much on how many customers we have but how many products and services are suitable for those customers that we do have. It's an issue of leverage. The more products and services that we can provide to a customer, the more difficult it is for him to leave, or even entertain leaving, because he's so intertwined with our company. That means long-term growth and security.

Who We Avoid

Then, obviously enough, there's the other side of the coin—those people with whom we're certain the chemistry is going to go sour. And it often boils down to several short words:

"Me." "Myself." "I." Never "us," "we," "them," or other terms that suggest respect and a commitment to cooperation.

They're easy enough to spot—the guys who dominate a conversation by talking only about themselves, what they want, expect, or even demand, without the slightest recognition that there are other people who are also part of the equation.

This can go in a variety of tangents. There will be some guys who talk about how many people they've gone through, about the number of employees who have come and gone. Maybe they talk about relationships with subcontractors that went bad. (In the end, that's no big surprise.)

Boiled down, it hints at a lack of flexibility and willingness to work together and cooperate. If people are only locked in on working a certain way, that's fine, but chances are excellent they won't be working with us.

In fact, in our experience, as a prospect gets to know us, it becomes as evident to him as it is to us whether we're going to build a solid relationship or not. Our process naturally highlights points of similarities and differences, so much so that everyone involved in the conversation knows the likelihood of a good fit. It's very much a two-way process. It works very, very well for us because, in the end, we want customers to fall in love with the process, not just the product. In this case, the process is our working relationship.

This is more than just a matter of targeting people with whom we feel confident we can work. If you're not truly selective about your customers, you can end up compromising your integrity. You start bending your principles, making decisions you might not otherwise even consider. In effect, you start working for them, rather than them working for you as well.

If you give it some thought, that makes sense. Sure, we're providing them with valuable products and services but, in return, they're boosting the growth of our business—and, in the process, reinforcing the values we believe in. That's what we mean by them working for us.

If you try to build that kind of relationship with someone who's only focused on himself, it's bound to fall apart quickly. A two-way street is only drivable if the drivers on both sides of the road are comfortable in their lanes. If someone swerves, you have to as well. And, in business, that can mean compromising your reputation or values, which is something we've never done and never will. We won't sacrifice principles or integrity for profit, and the people with whom we work know that. Chances are you feel the same way.

Leading with "the Core"

This leads to the obvious question: if we know the kind of customer we'd like to work with, what do we do to win them over to doing business with us?

We always lead with what we're really good at: that one core competency. And that boils down to making people feel comfortable and gaining their confidence. We care about how we look. We care about how we talk. We care about how we act and the kind of impression that we leave with others—in our business there are very few guys who do that!

Well, maybe we should say there used to be very few companies focused on professionalism and impressions. Our industry is currently undergoing a significant paradigm shift. And frankly, they're riding our coattails. The second and third generations that are taking over for Dad are starting to care about image, professionalism, and education. They have stopped spouting the old line, "That's how my dad did it," and started to realize that the way their dad ran the business wasn't necessarily right in today's business environment.

From there, we add on the "sidecar." We start bolting on those services and different components that make us really hard to leave or divorce. They're not necessarily our core, but they're essential in their own right.

They're valuable not just of their importance to a particular project, but to our relationship with our customers. Our competitors will always come in with a cheaper price. Always. We charge a very fair price for our service, but one thing that all our customers always get is an extra person on their staff. That comes in the form of our expertise. We get emails and phone calls on a weekly basis from customers asking questions they should be asking their architects and engineers. That's the kind of broad level of expertise that we have, and customers immediately recognize the value of that insight—experience and knowledge they don't have to pay extra for.

When approaching a customer, be sure to lead with your strength, but don't overlook other attractive services, features, and aspects that not only differentiate you from your competitors but, over time, make customers want to come back to you, time and time again—in fact, they even need to come back. You're that irreplaceable.

"It's Not Personal, It's Business"—It's Bullshit

Inherent in our approach to the care and feeding of customers is disproving an old saying: "It's not personal, it's business." To which we say: bullshit.

From our perspective, there's no such thing as business on one side and personal on the other. It's all together, and there's no way to separate them.

On one level, that comes back to how we choose customers and make other business decisions. We make decisions based on our gut. We make decisions based on our heart. We also make decisions based on our head, but we do them collectively and we do them as a group because everyone in our nest has a different perspective. That leads to really good solutions.

But, as we've discussed, we also develop these very close, very tight-knit relationships with customers. That's because we don't separate business and the personal. When you get to that place where you have a personal bond with a customer, there's a sense of obligation. There's a genuine connection. Nobody ever wants to let anyone down—again, the two-way relationship that we touched on earlier.

In one respect, that personal bond can be somewhat conventional. Still, it does take effort. We take the time to remember wives' names, kids' names, where a customer last went on a vacation. Sometimes, those personal bonds can take you in some funky directions. We know personal details about some of our customers that we don't condone in any way, but we keep that to ourselves, nonetheless. Granted, we don't dangle that knowledge in front of anyone, but it's the eight-hundred-pound gorilla in the corner that we both know about. That tends to keep business relationships together, because they know they can trust you. Looked at another way, you never let anyone down—your customers, your business partners, your employees, and particularly yourself. Standing room only, yet again.

A Guide to Feeding a Customer

OK, so you've got a customer on board. They're a great fit. They're precious. How do you take care of them?

The first key is communication. Answer the phone. Respond to the customer whether it's good news, bad news, no news, or whatever. Let them know you're being attentive to them, regardless of the situation.

These days, an all-too-pervasive problem is that nobody answers their phones. Nobody gets back to you in a timely manner. You're trying to iron out important scheduling details for a project—what do you eventually hear back?

Sorry we didn't call. We're really busy.

That's the second rule of customer feeding. Being busy is not an excuse in our organization for not responding promptly to a customer. It's simply not, and it shouldn't be in yours. If you think about it, you'd better be busy or you don't have a company. In effect, you're telling your customers: "We're really successful, so we don't have time for you." We don't think that's the message that anyone intends to send, but there it is.

Additionally, make the most of time you spend with each and every customer. By that, we mean taking the time to really listen to what customers are saying. If you're face to face, check out body language. Is a customer saying he's satisfied when his expression and body movement suggest he's really pissed off about something?

It's more than identifying problems. When you listen to them and pick out those things that they want, you can provide an extra touch that says you're thoughtful. You're creative. You go the extra mile. You're offering suggestions and ideas that really resonate.

As we hinted at earlier in this chapter, that's also a differentiator. Many businesses do all the traditional schmoozing, like taking customers out for a steak dinner. That's accepted practice, but it doesn't always address what the customer wants you to hear—what, in fact, you *need* to hear. That puts you in the position to anticipate and to perform. And all the steak dinners in the world won't make up for a lack of performance. As soon as you stop performing, your customers start looking around for someone who will.

Firing a Customer

In the years we've been running our business, we've routinely turned down jobs—many of them rather lucrative. Since we have a system and philosophy in place to find the right sort of customer for us, we've had outstanding success in developing long-term relationships with people who work for us as much as we work for them. That means occasionally saying thanks but no thanks.

It hasn't been flawless. On occasion, we've started work with a customer only to realize that, in fact, the fit simply isn't there. Often, the reason is that they forgot why they wanted to do business with us in the first place. Maybe they begin to overlook the value of two-way communication. They won't answer emails or phone calls.

It can be of a more personal nature. Maybe someone calls and treats someone in our company disrespectfully. That doesn't work for us at all. Supersized egos that look to climb up by stepping on others have no place with us.

Of course, it's not necessarily a one strike and you're out arrangement. Depending on the specifics, we'll give customers second chances to act in a different way or to mend fences if need be. But, a second chance is pretty much it. If a customer continues to act and behave in a way we simply don't tolerate, we fire them.

That may seem like a harsh, even reckless thing to do—after all, if someone's acting poorly but still scratching checks, what sense does it make to tell him to take a walk? Simple: sooner or later, it's going to fall apart. Far better and less painful to recognize what exists and to move on as quickly as possible.

As unlikely as it may seem, it all works out in the end. In our eyes, we're batting a thousand, both in the customers with whom we've developed solid, long-term relationships as well as those whom we let go. We have never once fired a customer, only to regret the decision later on. That's because we know the kind of customer who fits with our business, plain and simple.

The means with which we fire a customer are pretty straightforward. Generally, we get on the phone with them, begin chatting, and simply come out with what we have to say. This relationship isn't working out. It's tapping our resources. Many thanks for your business, but we simply are not going to be moving forward.

What happens after that can be a bit awkward, at least on the other end of the line. There are usually a few moments of silence while the customer processes what he's just been told. After that, they'll often become upset ("This is the first time I've ever been fired in my life!"). But we stick to our guns. Sorry it had to be this way, but that's our deal. Good luck to you in the future.

Of course, we don't enjoy doing this—who does? (By the way, if you do enjoy firing others—or, at the very least, it never bothers you in the least—you may want to step back and consider your mindset. It may not be healthy.) But, in the end, it's important to recognize your customer profile and, if need be, to make tough decisions that are in line with your integrity and philosophy. It's best for your business and probably best for the customer as well.

One Uncomfortable Thing Every Day

For many, the thought of "firing" a customer may be very unsettling. We get that. Naturally, you don't feel good doing it. But it's a necessary kind of discomfort.

One way we've learned to handle it better is through a simple exercise: do one uncomfortable thing every day. Maybe it's as simple as talking with someone who's always intimidated you or something more outlandish like getting into a crowded elevator and turning around and staring at everyone else!

Why do this? It helps you grow. You move beyond the cocoon of your regular comfort zone. You become more at ease doing things that might have been completely impossible before. In a way, you learn to embrace discomfort.

That's valuable when it comes time to fire a customer. Again, it's no one's idea of the best time you've ever had. It's difficult. But, in acclimating yourself to discomfort, you handle it better—in effect, making things easier and more professional for both you and your customer. That can only further cement a positive, straightforward reputation.

Chapter Six

Financial Discipline

Your business is up and running. You've got a great team in place. Even better, you're beginning to make money—real money.

As we say around here, don't smile just yet.

It may seem a weird thing to suggest, but making money can often prove the downfall of your business—if you don't know how to handle it properly once you've got it in your hands.

That leads to our second turn of phrase: learn first, earn second. Put another way, far better to know how best to handle your money before the time comes to actually do it.

You've Got Just Eleven Months

We'll never forget the first time we received a check at Xpro. It was $417,000. We'd honestly never seen a check that big.

What to do? Buy a '48 Hatteras and name it "Big Pimpin"? A down payment on a Gulfstream 6? A bronze statue of myself?

No, cautioned Jay. After running some calculations, taking into account taxes, expenses, and other issues, he pointed out that $417,000 would keep us afloat for the next eleven months, based on the possibility that we didn't land another job within that timeframe. In eleven months, we would be flat broke.

Take a look at how we phrased that. It wasn't, "We're solid for nearly a year!" No, instead it was: "Just eleven months? We better get off our asses and start working!"

That's the kind of mindset we can't emphasize enough. Sure, making money is great—especially when it shows up in the form of nearly half a mil—but it can blind you to reality. And that reality is that your finances are only so secure until that next paycheck comes along. In the meantime, get out there and hustle and make sure that the money that's already in your pocket lasts as long as possible.

The formula we used wasn't unnecessarily complicated. In a nutshell, it was basically a certain percentage of living expenses plus a certain percentage of business expenses pro-rated by the money that we had on hand. If you want to be as accurate as possible, have your accountant run the calculation.

But, however it happens, do it. Looking at money that you have in terms of lifespan rather than a blank check for all sorts of tempting goodies can make all the difference between building an extraordinary business or one that stumbles from one paycheck to the next—or worse.

Ten Times Twelve Doesn't Mean 120

In talking about taking this different mindset toward what money you earn, it's also important to point out a natural tendency that many of us have. Let's say you earn $10,000 in a particular month. Human nature leads you to extrapolate that, since I earned $10k this month, that means I'm going to make $120,000 for the year. Simple math.

Simple and understandable, but also misleading for anyone who's in business for themselves.

That's a short-term viewpoint that can be very dangerous. For one thing, you're basically operating on an assumption that can prove pretty unreliable in real life. Sure, you made $10,000 this month. Where's it cast in stone that next month will bring another $10,000?

We can attest to this. We've had months where we've made $80,000 apiece. We've also had months where we've made $3,000 apiece. There have been months when we are able to take out nice, big sums to spend on our families. There have been others when we haven't even been near the bank, let alone withdrawing anything for ourselves. Simply put, we pay ourselves based on what we've brought in.

This isn't meant to be some sort of downer message. Rather, it's meant to be real and utterly practical. By playing it close to the vest and making sure that you use a disciplined approach to your money, not only will you grow your business, you'll also be able to enjoy the rewards of your labor with a good deal less to worry about.

Surfing as an Example of Cash Flow

The first thing you do is paddle out, sit on your board, and wait for the wave that you like. You jump on that wave and you ride it in. When your tailfin drags on the ground, you jump off the board, you paddle back out, and you grab another one. Repeat.

But what happens when there are no waves? You just sit out there, hoping that conditions are going to change. Sometimes they do, sometimes they don't. And you don't have a thing to say about it. That's an issue of unforeseen circumstances—something you have zero control over.

That's the way we approach our business. There are no sure things and you have to approach it from that perspective. A big check that arrives today may be the last one you see for a while—hopefully not, but far better to look at it in that framework. We don't do it out of fear, we do it because we recognize that as reality. And, going back to the surfing example one more time, when that big wave finally does come around, the ride in is all the more sweet. And, for that matter, potentially dangerous—high reward carries high risk. Don't lose sight of that equation, no matter how appealing the ride might be.

Practice Living Poor

Don't misunderstand. We've never been genuinely poor by any stretch of the imagination. But we have practiced living as though we were, and that's made a huge difference, both in our business and in our personal lives.

What does that mean? Of course, it means keeping a close eye on every dime we spend, every single expense. But there are other ways to learn to live below your means by practicing to be poor.

As business owners, one way to practice being poor is to avoid putting yourself on salary. We've seen this any number of times and, once again, it's understandable. A business is running reasonably well and the owner wants a degree of security and predictability when it comes to income. So he sets up a regular salary arrangement for himself—so much money paid out on a prescheduled basis. (This also refers back to the $10,000 times twelve months calculation we mentioned earlier—an assumption many owners take as a lock-solid certainty that's anything but.)

We understand that guys have bills, expenses, houses, and families. But it ignores the realities that we've been discussing—that you can't rely on income from one month to the next and that unintended expenses can crop up all the time. That's why it's better to pay yourself based on a percentage of profit, just as we do. That way, you only get what is reasonable and fair without financially jeopardizing yourself or your company.

Let's take the discussion of unpredictability a step further. Let's say you're in the construction-related business like us. What happens if it rains every day in the month of May? You're sitting on your hands waiting for the weather to improve, but you still have bills to pay. Where's the money going to come from?

Remember when we talked about the dangers of being too successful? That applies here as well. What if it's sunny every day in May and business is off the charts? All your people are double timing to keep up with the work demand. Great, but you still have to pay them (all the more if they're putting in overtime). How are you going to pay them for work done in May when you have to wait sixty days to be paid by all those customers? What if that carries over into the summer—you're growing all the time, but receivables can't catch up to meet the expenses that come with that kind of success?

The importance of practicing to be poor also relates to your own workload as boss. Consider: You're putting in sixty, maybe seventy hours a week, and you've been doing it for more months in a row than you care to count. You're constantly exhausted and stressed. What to do? Hire someone to help reduce your workload, of course.

Again, that's perfectly understandable—also, potentially financially disastrous. Business owners have a nasty habit of making new hires their first reaction to many problems rather than walking through their strategy to determine if a new hire really makes sense. A lot of business owners add people to their company because it makes their life easier. Who wouldn't love that? The problem is it increases your overhead without any related increase in income to justify the added expense. Plus, it can be habit forming—add one person, then another, and so on. The result is your workload may be less but your overhead has suddenly become enormous. Far better to add people when they're genuinely needed from a financial perspective—when your business, in effect, "allows" you to hire more people.

Rick's Story: a Great Partnership Always Helps

By now, it's obvious that Jay and I have a fantastic working relationship. But it goes beyond our day-to-day interaction—through Jay, I've learned the sorts of financial strategies and concepts that have allowed our business to blossom the way it has. My deal has always been on the top line of the business—sales—but Jay is a truly adept money manager. Many of the ideas I've learned—such as the ones we're sharing with you in this chapter—I might have had to learn the hard way were it not for Jay.

To put that in perspective, have you ever considered why those doomsday financial ads are on in the middle of the night: "I can help you with your tax liens from the IRS!" or "Need cash quick? Be approved in as little as twenty-four hours!" The reason they're on TV then is that they know their audience: all those people, many of whom are business owners, who are so freaking stressed out about money that they can't even think about sleep!

I think I'll take my "education" with Jay any day of the week— and sleep like a baby at night.

Negotiate, Then Negotiate Again

Part of being as smart about your finances as possible is negotiating the best deal possible on everything and anything.

That's not news. What is news is, once you've had a deal in place for a while, consider negotiating again. It's a simple rule of thumb: Renegotiate everything all the time. Never get complacent.

Backing up a bit, a lot of companies experience complacency in their purchasing habits and practices. They buy insurance, then just set it aside. They hire a CPA and leave it at that. They find a supplier and sign on. On the surface, it makes sense: once you've settled on something, move on to the next task at hand.

That can prove an expensive habit. For instance, we had our insurance coverage with one company for years. We just switched carriers. We saved thousands in the process. That's something we probably should have done a while back because we could have saved even more, but at least we finally came around to realize that we were simply paying more than we needed to.

That's an example of smart spending but it also pays to renegotiate other expenses, such as labor, research, or whatever costs that may benefit from ongoing attention. For instance, contact your vendors every six months and see if they'd be willing to adjust their charges. Ask about early payment discounts. Not only can that keep you on top of shopping for the best deals possible, but it also makes you aware of creeping expenses—incremental price increases that vendors can slip in with little or no fanfare. Pay no attention and, in a year or two, those incremental price hikes really add up. Keeping them in your sights and being ready to pursue new pricing structures and options can save you big time.

Be sure to stay on top of your customer payment terms as well. It can be tempting to be the "nice guy" who's reasonably open about when bills can be paid, but that's a lit fuse looking for a charge of dynamite. Instead, take the time to negotiate—and, if need be, renegotiate—payment terms that are simple, straightforward, and immune to any sort of misrepresentation. That way, you get a firm handle on when you can expect to receive money due you and plan accordingly in terms of both your short- and long-term cash needs.

Make the Bank Your Partner

Complacency can take hold in your relationship with your bank—unless, of course, you choose instead to make your bank your bitch.

When we started out, we walked in and literally opened a checking account with a local bank based on a referral from a friend. Although they were happy to take our money, we meant absolutely nothing to them. That's understandable to a point. Banks like to see a track record. They want to see growth.

They certainly saw that with us. Over the first couple of years we opened up more accounts and deposited more money. The bank noticed the cash flow and came to us asking what lending needs we might have. Did we need an equipment lease? They helped us with that. Did we need a loan for a new building? No problem.

So, on one level, it's best just to be patient and grow with the bank. Eventually, you can get to a point with a bank where it's a press of a button. Need something? No worries.

But like businesses handling their necessary purchases, banks can also become complacent. That's exactly what happened with us. Our bank figured they had us locked up tight; we weren't going anywhere. Not true: we eventually ended up taking our banking needs elsewhere. Not only were we rewarded with the sort of attention and responsiveness that we deserved, we also saved some thousands in costs by taking our banking contract to someone else.

The bottom line here is watch for complacency on both ends of a relationship. True, you can become complacent and lose money on contracts and other arrangements that you simply don't pay enough attention to, but the same can be said for a bank that mistakenly assumes there's nowhere else you can take your business. If they balk, don't be afraid to look around. You'll be saving money and headaches while your former bank is out looking for last year's Easter eggs.

Need a Bank? Hold an Interview

The stereotypic view of a banking relationship is one where the bank holds all the cards. You go there, hat in hand, and plead with them to give you a loan or a line of credit. If you're one of the lucky ones, they deign to meet your needs.

It doesn't have to be that way. And it starts by interviewing a bank just as you would interview any prospective employee or business partner.

Admittedly, a lot of people are afraid to qualify or interview a bank. It's understandable. They always feel like—and we used to feel like this—that you're the one being interviewed, not the other way around.

Flip that on its head. When you meet with a banking representative, be ready with a long list of questions for them. What are you going to do for us? How much is the bank worth? How do you run your company? What is your short- and long-term outlook? Do you expect to be acquired by someone else and, if so, how will that affect your lending procedures?

The idea is to make it more of a 50-50 arrangement. They want to see your financials? Tell them you want to see *their* financials. Have them tell you about types of customers they serve. Like other aspects of running a business that we've already covered, is there a cultural "fit"? Do they share the same priorities and values that you have?

Ask about the mechanics of their business. How large an amount of funding can the president or a loan officer approve without taking it to the board? If the board comes into play, will that amount increase and by how much? How quickly can you expect a decision if a request has to go before the board?

Leverage the dynamics of the market just as any prospective customer might leverage them with you. If a bank doesn't meet your needs or requirements or becomes complacent, don't ignore the fact that there's somebody right down the street who'll be happy to pick you up. In the end, the bank ends up working for you—not the other way around. Just as important, it knows full well what's necessary to keep you satisfied.

Is It Raining? Let's Go on a Picnic!

It's not surprising that financial issues are the primary cause of most business failures. What we hope we've conveyed in this chapter is that many—if not most—of those financial snafus are avoidable.

It boils down to an overriding commitment to discipline: the discipline to treat income as a call to action to keep hustling. Like we said, don't smile just yet. The discipline to avoid a salary structure that's not in line with your financial reality. The discipline to be diligent about watching expenses with an ongoing attention to renegotiation. The discipline to craft your relationship with your bank more as a partnership—one where the onus on performance is as much on the bank as it is on you. The discipline to learn first and earn later.

As we said, it's amazing how many of these financial problems can be skirted with careful planning and disciplined execution. It's like planning a picnic, in a way.

We've all heard those dark statistics about business failures. While they vary a good deal, one suggests that four out of five businesses will eventually go under.

Flip that statistic over to another setting. Would you plan a picnic when there was a four out of five chance that you'd be rained out?

Hell no. You'd plan your picnic for another time when the weather was more to your liking.

Treat your business finances the same way. Like heading out for a picnic where you hope the weather holds, don't just hope to be the business that bucks survival statistics. Plan to be the exception.

Chapter Seven

The Idiots Out There

They're out there—lots of them. And if you want your business to grow and prosper, you'd better know how to deal with them.

We're talking about the idiots. In the business world, you're likely going to run into a hell of a lot of them.

They're not just an annoying pain in the ass—they can be a real problem, an ongoing struggle. That's because idiots are often in a position of influence, which can prove a real danger to your business.

Don't be tempted to just shrug them off. It's critical that you're ready to handle them as effectively as possible. Experience has showed us that, not only are there idiots out there around every corner, but you also need a strategy to deal with them as effectively as possible. Otherwise, your business is going to suffer. Worse, it may compromise your professionalism.

Idiot Engineering 101

The first thing to know about the idiots who can derail your business is the various types you're likely to encounter. They're all over the place—in accounts payable, customer service, sales, managers, vice presidents, you name it. They're hiding everywhere and you may not notice they're there until you're in the thick of a job with them.

Potential idiots:

- **The stealth idiot.** He seems smart and shows a willingness to work together but, once things get rolling, he starts to show his true colors, trying to impede progress and your success whenever and however he can.

- **The classic front-line idiot**. These guys are more up front about their idiocy. They make no effort to gloss over their belief that it's their way or the highway—no cooperation, no give and take whatsoever. This idiot is in plain sight.

Both idiots are very secure in what they do. If you try to go around them, you lose. If, like we tried with our first job, you try to deal with them directly and in a straightforward manner, you're going to lose. That's particularly true in a vendor relationship such as ours.

What to do? We created something called Idiot Engineering 101—a complete, step-by-step process on what to do when you uncover an idiot:

- **Step One: Make sure you're not the idiot**. Let's be honest—sometimes we all lash out at others or look for open wounds because of our own shortcomings, fears, anger, or just hoping to pin mistakes on others. So, if you look in the mirror and see you're the idiot, that's half the battle. Recognize what you're doing as an idiot and takes steps to correct it and, if necessary, make amends.

- **Step Two: Cut some slack**. You're not the idiot? Great. Now, be sure to go easy on the one who is the idiot. Cut him a break, because most idiots are in over their heads. That's the number one cause of idiocy. Or, maybe there are personal problems—a divorce, issues with their kids—that are causing them to act the way they're acting. Of course, that may not be the case at all—some idiots come by it naturally—but start out by giving them the benefit of the doubt.

- **Step Three: Devise a strategy.** This is where it gets tricky, but can be simple: pay attention to an idiot's interests. If there's a signed football on his desk, bring up football. If there's a book around, ask about the author. Talk about what interests them and play to a personal side. That can encourage a tendency on their part to care a little more about other things—such as the job you're working on together. Don't misunderstand. This isn't kissing ass—not in the least. To overcome an idiot, try to blend your ideas with theirs, find common ground.

- **Step Four: Know the positive signs.** Common ground can lead to an idiot actually listening to some of your suggestions. If an idiot adopts one of your ideas as his own, you know you're on the right track. If they want to feel like they're the smartest person in the room, go ahead and let them. At least you know the idea they're saying is theirs is solid—after all, it really came from you.

- **Step Five: Don't play their game.** However tempting it might be, it's essential not to get sucked into an idiot's vortex. Don't try to throw anybody under the bus; don't look to bad mouth someone behind their back. The next thing you know, you're as big an idiot as he is. That's what we meant about compromising your professionalism.

- **Step Six: Don't burn bridges.** The objective in dealing with idiots isn't to play their games or bring someone down. The goal is to make things work. Accordingly, don't burn any bridges when it comes to dealing with an idiot. An idiot that's in one job at one point in time can resurface somewhere else, perhaps in a company that you're prospecting or with which you already have a relationship. Again, focus on making things work.

- **Step Seven: Overcommunicate.** Communication is a solid idea, regardless of whom you're dealing with. All the more so with an idiot. Keep communication lines open. Answer emails quickly. Try to stay ahead as much as possible so things don't have a chance to fester, however inadvertently. If delegating responsibility, place your best communicator and your best listener on the jobs where an idiot plays a prominent role.

- **Step Eight: Did I get that right?** Idiots rarely pick up on the fact that they're acting like idiots. One of the ways to help them see that is to lay out exactly what they're saying so they can see it for themselves.

Hiring an Idiot

We're justifiably proud of our record in hiring the right people for the right jobs. But, like everyone else, we're not perfect. Everyone, including us, is going to have moments of idiocy. Everyone, sooner or later, is going to screw up at some point—particularly if you empower them with the autonomy to use their best judgment and make decisions, often difficult ones.

When someone acts like an idiot inside your company, don't go off the deep end and scream and rant. Instead, sit down with them and point out where they went wrong so they don't repeat the same mistake. If you empower people, you can't holler at them any time their judgment leads them to the wrong decision.

The message here is that idiots can be both outside your company as well as within. If they're employees, it's essential to expect screw-ups from time to time. Be patient and do what's necessary to correct them. Moreover, put the right people in the right jobs so they're positioned to succeed as much as possible.

Take the Path of Least Resistance

One of the interesting things about dealing with idiots in a professional setting is the surprise many of us experience. After all, we deal with idiots in every other area of our lives—what is it about encountering an idiot in a position of authority? It makes you wonder: how did this idiot get this job and, just as bewildering, how does he stay there?

Unfortunately, those aren't particularly productive questions. Idiots can attain—and retain—a job for all sorts of reasons, often with very little to do with competence. Trying to figure out how an idiot got a certain job and has kept it is merely spinning your wheels. What matters is that they're there.

If the idiot in question has a business relationship with you, terminating the relationship is always one option—although we always think it's a good idea to wait a little bit to see if the idiot improves or is removed.

But sometimes that's not possible. Maybe the idiot has been in the job forever and, for whatever reason, his bosses think he's doing just fine. Or maybe the idiot doesn't have a real impact on your business but is more of an annoyance, nothing more than a pain in the ass.

In those instances, merely going with the flow may be your best option. Live with the idiot and his idiotic ways as best you can with the least bit of anguish. Of course, if the idiot is negatively impacting your business, you can end the relationship. But, if the idiot is just, well, an idiot with little effect on what you do, better to expend your energy on other things.

Here's an example of what we mean. We work with a company whose mail run is at 3:15 p.m. The checks they write us are often very substantial, so at first we tried to get to the company to pick them up rather than having to wait for them to arrive in the mail.

Enter idiot stage left. If we tell the person handling the checks that we'll have someone there at 3:20 or 3:30 to pick up the check, that check has already gone into the mail at 3:15. No exceptions. God forbid they hold the check for an extra five or ten minutes. And, by the same token, if you show up early at 2:45, you're turned away. The checks aren't ready yet.

Okay: Note to ourselves. Let's not bother trying to pick up the checks at Idiot Junction again. Let the mail take care of that. Sometimes, trying to work with an idiot is simply hopeless. Move on and let them wallow in their idiocy.

The core message here is that every idiot is situational. Some may be open to change, some you're better off with no relationship at all, and some you just live with as best as possible. It's your decision—do what feels right for you.

And, never forget: the battle is fierce but it's all in how you handle it.

Idiots are inevitable, but they don't have to be terminal.

An Idiot Cheat Sheet

As a reference, here's a quick guide of ideas and strategies that can help you resolve a variety of issues, not just with idiots but with anyone with whom you have a disagreement.

- Don't blame.

- Attack the problem, not the person.

- Communicate how you feel assertively, not aggressively.

- Focus on the issue, not on your position about the issue.

- Accept that opinions differ.

- Work to develop common ground.

- Don't force compliance.

- Listen without interrupting.

- If only one person is satisfied in a conflict, it is not resolved and will continue.

- Forget the past and stay in the present.

- Build "power with" not "power over" others.

- Always thank the person for listening.

Abraham Lincoln once said: "The best way to defeat an enemy is to make him a friend."

Here's to making lots of friends in your future.

Chapter Eight

Teambuilding

Peⁿ ople who launch their own businesses are naturally self-confident. They have to be. Starting, growing, and nurturing your own business requires major stones—just a look at the failure rate of new businesses is enough to frighten away more than a few would-be entrepreneurs.

That said, business owners can be a little delusional when it comes to looking after certain aspects of their business. To be blunt: they're doing stuff they shouldn't be doing. They want to be the accountant and they want to be the attorney (thankfully, they can't be the banker!).

Still, they want to wear all these hats and, in the process, save a few bucks. That's fine, but it's also a good way to run your business into the ground.

That means it makes all the sense in the world to build a team of outside experts and advisors. But it's not just a matter of finding the people with the most expertise, although that's certainly important. It's also valuable to build a team that fits your particular culture, because you're going to need guys who are like minded and with whom you can talk. In the end, you'll get a lot more done and be a lot more productive.

Four Essential Horsemen

We were initially recommended to our first accountant. Even though the recommendation was enthusiastic, we still interviewed him—an important step that you should take when it comes to finding all of your key horsemen, no matter if they work directly for you or indirectly. You need to know if there's a cultural fit. For instance, can we float a funny joke to our accountant about cheating on our taxes without him scolding us for it?

As it turns out, our first accountant was this very dry, straight kind of guy. He wasn't warm, to say the least. But he was keeping things tight and very structured, and that's kind of what we wanted in the early days.

Like our accountant, we were also referred to a banker when we first started out. It was an entirely different experience. We immediately hit it off with the general manager of the bank. He was very likeminded and understood our culture. He understood our personalities. We knew from the get-go that he was the right fit for us.

Our attorney and insurance guy followed pretty much the same patterns. The basic, underlying question when we started out was: will this guy get our personalities? As we'll get into in a bit, there were other criteria that we used in choosing our horsemen, but the cultural and personality fit was always at the basis of the search.

Bear in mind, too, that none of these guys was full time. They were relatively insignificant to us because there was very little substance to our business. We were just getting started. The accountant was on a small retainer and we were paying him very little. We had no relationship with the bank because we had no money in the bank. Our relationship with our lawyer was largely limited to articles of incorporation—we weren't suing anyone or getting sued, so there was little for him to do.

Growth, Then Change

Our relationship with our horsemen started to change when we began gaining traction as a business. We started to grow, we added employees, and we started to make more money. And, as we started to grow, we became our accountant's biggest customer. We became our bank's biggest customer. We became much more involved with our insurance agent because we were dealing with a number of smaller companies with different insurance requirements. By contrast, we never really needed a lawyer until last year when we got tangled up in a lawsuit. Now, we have a lawyer on retainer.

But, if there's any downside to growth, it's the change that it can bring about in your relationship with your horsemen. In our case, we grew so quickly at first we weren't aware of the changing nature of those relationships. Simply put, you need to know if you've out-grown your horsemen, whether you've grown to the point where you're much bigger than the company you keep.

Our first accountant is an ideal example. When we first signed on with him, we were looking for an accountant who was going to save us money on our taxes. That was our first strategy. We wanted a guy who was going to be aggressive, to get us all the tax relief that we were legally entitled to. Also, we wanted a consultant, someone who would spot money-saving ideas and bring our attention to them.

Eventually, though, we realized that we had pushed our accountant to the limits of what he could do. We were too complex for what he was able to provide. We were given a referral to a large accounting firm in Nashville, and we started the process all over again. We eventually had a comprehensive two-hour interview to find out what their capacities were. As part of the process, we also learned that we were doing some things wrong from a financial standpoint. For instance, we had incorrectly designated a portion of our business in terms of financial status.

We also came to understand the scope of what a properly matched accounting firm could do for us. They have been able to counsel us, to provide ideas, and to stay ahead of us in terms of monitoring our financials.

Put simply, our prior accountant tended to react. These guys are utterly proactive. They're providing us with the documentation that we need to fill out and send in. They're providing us the consultation that we need to keep moving forward.

The bottom line here is that you constantly need to be upgrading your horsemen with your business. If the company that you are currently using cannot upgrade or does not have the capacity to upgrade, then you need to find somebody else.

Watch for Complacency

Of course, reading this, you may be tempted to say that our new accounting firm is just a bigger expense than our prior one. The truth is, they may cost more, but we may not actually be paying more. The advice they give us and the guidance they offer may be worth far more than any additional amount they may be charging.

That's not to say to take your horsemen's fees on simple blind faith. Anything but. In the case of our first accountant, we really didn't understand his fee structure. We'll never forget the first bill we got! Jay immediately called the owner of the accounting firm and said we needed to review this because this is not what we talked about. You can't be nervous about asking for fee clarifications and, if necessary, to question bills.

Accountants, attorneys, and insurance companies charge businesses for all sorts of services and they pay because that's what they're supposed to do. But it's okay to negotiate these rates. It's okay to say you quoted me $195 an hour and you charged me $250. It's okay to say to your insurance agent that you noticed a 20 percent rate increase—is there another company you represent that you can obtain a rate from so we can get a better deal?

This hints at another issue to watch for: complacency. When you have advisors for a long period of time, it's natural that some complacency can set in. Things have gone perfectly fine up to now—why expend energy on a relationship that seems perfectly solid?

That can be a big mistake. Our insurance agency got complacent. We had been with them so long, they fell into a mentality that they didn't need to service us. They didn't feel the need to shop rates for us, even though, as we just mentioned, we had questioned why we were being hit with a 20 percent increase in a particular premium.

We switched insurance companies and saved thousands a year. And we switched not just because of the money saved but because the insurance company had become complacent. They were taking us for granted. As a result, they lost our business.

They're not alone. Our former bank just lost millions of dollars' worth of business because they got complacent—they put us at the bottom of the pile and assumed we weren't going anywhere. They also took us for granted. By contrast, our new bank has saved us tremendous amounts of money just by lowering our interest rate. They've provided us with very usable financial tools leveraging some of the assets we have to make important purchases. Our new banker cares about where we are today, but he's more excited about where we're going to be in five years.

We have a business to run just like anybody else. If you're reading this book you likely have a business of your own as well, and there's no room for complacency anywhere, any time. That means it's smart to continuously keep an eye out for complacency. Keep your horsemen honest to make certain they're not taking you for granted.

What Works—and What Doesn't

Your horsemen are charged with always looking out for your best interests. Sometimes, that may take the form of advice that, on the surface, isn't appealing in the least.

We recently had a little legal tangle. We knew we were in the right and we hired a lawyer to represent us to that end. The lawyer kept telling us that we would win with no problem at all—the other guys didn't have a leg to stand on.

But there was one problem. We didn't calculate how big the company was we were fighting, the resources that they had, and what they were willing to spend to fight us. From their perspective, they knew enough about us to know that they could outlast us financially.

In many ways, it was a battle of ego versus reality. On the one hand, our attorney was telling us we could win the lawsuit. But, it could take upwards of a year and cost us about $100,000. Still, we decided to fight on.

Not long into the proceedings, we got an offer from the plaintiff. Our attorney explained it would cost us only about $30,000 to settle. We also had to stay away from certain customers for about a year.

We thought about it some more and talked it over with our attorney. We discussed the $100,000 we would likely spend over a year or so trying to win versus only $30,000 and a small group of customers we'd have to stay away from for a short while. Our attorney recommended that we settle and put the whole thing behind us. We did, and he was absolutely right.

The point here is that solid horsemen know what's best for you at all times. And, occasionally, that may mean a few bruises to your ego. But a horseman who would have urged us to fight on no matter what—and continue to collect hefty fees as the process dragged out—wouldn't have been representing our best interests. And, sometimes, that can sting a little.

Other Shopping Tips

One of the first rules of thumb in choosing the right horsemen is to know their background. Check with any professional groups or oversight associations. Make sure they haven't been in any sort of trouble with the law. Check the bar association to make certain the lawyer is clean. Check the accountants association to make sure that the accountant is clean.

Check to see how well the bank is capitalized.

Additionally, look for horsemen who have experience in your particular field. If, for instance, an attorney has worked in our industry, he's going to naturally have insight and perspective that someone without that experience won't. He'll be able to anticipate problems and issues before they come up. Are they capable of understanding how your business works? If they're not, they'll be guessing. They'll be missing stuff.

Lastly, don't get wound up in what their office looks like. Don't get wound up in how cheap the suits are they're wearing. Instead, get wound up in the advice they're providing. Get wound up in the comfort that you have with them. We know people who are wound up by lawyers on the eighteenth floor in the biggest building downtown and drive the biggest Mercedes. That shouldn't matter in the least. As we mentioned earlier in the chapter, pay attention to their cultural fit, the vibe they give off. That matters a whole lot more than the fanciest office or biggest or most expensive car.

Care and Feeding

Like we said, it's important that your horsemen avoid becoming complacent. The same goes for you as well in the relationship.

Start with praise. Your accountant likes to be told he's doing a good job, your banker likes to be told he's doing a good job. They need to hear those things. They need to be told they're doing a good job because if they don't, they can feel as though you're taking them for granted, something that you wouldn't want them to do at any time. Telling your horsemen they're doing a good job and that you appreciate them tightens the relationship and makes them work a little harder for you.

To that end, it can be valuable to conduct annual reviews with each member of your team. In one respect, it gives you a chance to show your appreciation for all that they do. But it's also a check-up in other respects. Ask them for their take on where your business is headed and, from there, whether they can continue to do a good job for you. If they say absolutely, then you're okay. If they don't share your view of the future or hesitate in any way about their confidence in helping you get there, that can be a red flag. It can be time to start looking for a new horseman.

Protecting What's Yours

A solid horseman isn't an expense—it's an investment. No matter what he does, a well-chosen horseman will be there to guide you to help accelerate your success. That's not money down the drain— that's money put to work for the greater good of your business.

But, bear in mind the reality of a relationship with your horsemen. Even though they're an entrusted group of people, at the end of the day, they still do not have pictures of you and your family on their mantle.

That means it's important to have everything above board and in writing as much as possible. For instance, know your rights when you're talking to a lawyer. Attorney/client privacy is supposed to be iron clad, but it never hurts to make certain that's the case. It's okay to have these guys sign confidentiality agreements. As a matter of fact, every one of these guys we deal with has a confidentiality agreement. It's an important form of protection.

Yes, they're essential parts of your business and success. Yes, they're valuable guides. But, at the end of the day, it's about protecting what's yours, protecting your company, protecting your assets, protecting your cash, and protecting your employees. That's because of the commitment you've made to your employees and their families. Committed horsemen are important, but the commitment to your employees—and how the guidance and advice you get from your horsemen may impact them—is far more valuable.

$$\boxed{\textit{Chapter Nine}}$$

Leadership

We ended a prior chapter with an emphasis on always being aware of your responsibility to the people you employ.

Now, it's time to mention someone else you should never lose sight of: yourself.

No matter how valuable the varied people who make up your business are—and there's no doubting that—it's essential to remember at the end of the day, it's your name on the door.

How can you best look after your own interests? By honing your leadership skills as much as possible. Looked at another way, the best thing you can do for those who depend on you is to make yourself into the best leader you can become.

Performance—When No One's Watching

Think back to when you were a kid and your parents were keeping an eye on you. You were probably a perfect angel, right? You were well mannered, polite, and respectful to everyone around you.

That likely changed when Mom and Dad weren't around. You may have fought with your siblings, snatched food from the fridge that was supposed to be off limits, and even dropped a few F-bombs. You were a completely different kid.

Take that dynamic and apply it to your workplace. Think about when you walk through a work area. Everyone's focused on the job at hand, communicating, supporting each other. Now try to imagine what that scene is like when you're back in your office with the door shut.

Hopefully, the dynamics aren't different in the least. But they might be. And that comes down to the leadership you display—your ability to encourage, support, and build such a strong sense of pride and ownership in your employees that doing their best only when the boss is around doesn't even enter their minds.

Jay's Story: "When No One's Watching"

I remember one high school wrestling coach of mine very well. Not only was he a terrific coach, he also often said things that I remember to this day. He was very inspiring and always made you think. One year, at the season-ending banquet, he presented me with a plaque. It was inscribed: "Pride is the force that compels a man to do his very best even when no one is watching."

That's the attitude we've encouraged in our workplace. Our employees take genuine pride in what they do and, as Rick and I can tell you, we don't need to be watching over the shoulders to know they're doing their very best. That's a level of buy-in and company culture you can't put a value on.

As it happens, as I write this, the 2016 Olympic Games in Rio are taking place. That very same coach who presented me with that plaque is there. He coaches his wife, who's a pole vaulter. She won a gold medal in the prior Olympics in London and she's in Rio competing again!

I guess this former coach of mine is remarkable in building a winning attitude, no matter if no one's looking or there are millions of people around the world paying attention.

Why Others Follow a Leader: Three Causes

This discussion begs an obvious question: what is it about a leader that encourages others to follow him? From our perspective, there are three primary reasons, one of which isn't positive in the least.

Let's get that one out of way: fear of retribution. The mindset of "If I don't do what this guy says, I may lose my job." This is obviously the most unhealthy attitude an employee can have. In fact, it's hard to even call it a type of leadership: following out of fear is not so much following as being dragged along at the end of a rope. Nor is it built to last, as fear works only so long as the follower sees no other choice.

Not only is fear a tool that truly effective leaders avoid, it also builds weak commitment and needs constant attention. People who follow out of fear aren't built for the long term. If nothing else, they're likely to jump ship when an offer they see as "better" comes along.

Fortunately, those people are easy to identify. A follower in this situation is probably desperate for a solution, and what the leader is offering is either the only option they see or the best of a relatively weak set of choices. Consider: Are some employees agreeing to certain ideas and decisions that you suspect they really don't believe in? In your gut, do you think they'd truly like to speak up but are afraid of the consequences?

It's not a hopeless situation. If you notice someone who's following out of fear, don't be hesitant about telling him that fear isn't a healthy form of motivation. From there, offer to work with the employee to help build a different mindset and attitude. Often, that's little more than reviewing performance and, if necessary, making any recommendations or suggestions to improve any perceived problems. Often, once an employee is secure in the knowledge that he's doing a good job, following out of fear becomes completely moot.

The second reason is unqualified faith in the leader. They think: "What a great person. If anyone knows the answer, this guy does. I'm going to follow this guy because I believe that whatever he's going to do is going to work."

On the surface, this may seem like the ideal follower—one who bleeds absolute, unquestioned loyalty. But the problem is this sort of follower is blind to any sort of underlying reason and is merely following out of pure faith. He believes that the leader, by some wave of a magic wand or force or sheer genius, will always provide the right solution. That confidence may seem solid, but it's not based on substance.

Happily, there is something that you can build on with this sort of employee as well. They may have no basis for their faith in the leader, but they can be taught. Since their buy-in is obvious, they're open to learning just why that faith may be substantiated. They're ready and willing to understand the "why." So, share your company philosophy and mission statement. Encourage them to recognize genuine, practical reasons for confidence in your leadership.

The third and final follower is ideal. Here, there's intellectual agreement. This follower understands why the organization does what it does and embraces it. He grasps the logic and the solution. He knows if he follows you, he's going to be in a better position in the future. Moreover, there's an emotional commitment, a sense of real attachment. When a follower understands the leader's vision, he's emotionally close.

A true leader always works to build the mindset of the third sort of follower. Their attachment doesn't derive from fear or thoughtless acceptance. Instead, it's a response to the leader's ability to connect, communicate, and convey the overriding message that characterizes any successful business.

Steps to Great Leadership

As we said, encouraging people to always do their best regardless of the circumstances requires solid leadership. And, while some people are naturally great leaders, others become great leaders by constantly evaluating what they say, what they do, and building a solid list of leadership principles. Those guidelines are often overlooked but they're very straightforward and make a world of sense:

1. **Approach challenges together.** Show them that you're willing to get dirty. As we mentioned, if we're on a work site and we notice a truck needs unloading, we're ready to pitch in immediately and help. There's no standing on hierarchy in that kind of situation.

   But taking on challenges as a team means more than that. As a leader, be curious. Commit to listening to new ideas and insights. Establish the sort of team where everyone's input is valued and considered. The best leaders we've ever been around have been very curious and actively interested in all the things around them that pertain to their business.

2. **Create a positive environment.** This can go in any number of directions. For one thing, we're always looking out for toxic relationships—people whose attitudes and actions can compromise the spirit of our business. If we see someone whose behavior may have a negative impact, we often act very quickly to let them go. Misery loves company and, if you come across someone who's miserable in his work, better to have him share his misery elsewhere.

   A positive environment also comes through in what employees say and do. For instance, when employees know the strategic focus of the company and can articulate it, they're really starting to listen to you. They see how their position relates to the company and the company's strategic focus. This comes back to the "ideal" follower we discussed earlier—someone who

understands where the company is heading as well as
their role and value.

3. **Create an environment where people feel comfortable
   speaking up.** Here's a simple question: do your employees feel comfortable coming to you with questions
   or problems?

   That can be a dicey question for many businesses.
   For one thing, it's a given that, if many employees are
   loyal out of fear, they're certainly going to be the last
   ones to speak their minds. Even employees who are
   more comfortable in their situation may be gun-shy
   about expressing their opinions—not because of fear of
   being fired but, if nothing else, the feeling that whatever they have to say won't be taken seriously.

   Here's a situation that just occurred in our business. We had to let a particular employee go. Before
   we parted ways, he sent us a lengthy email that, on the
   surface, seemed to throw another employee completely
   under the bus—criticism, innuendo, you name it.

   Although we chalked much of it up to the emotion
   of the moment, we also realized that there were some
   grains of truth in what he said. It was a solid lesson
   for us: even though we have gone to great lengths
   to encourage our employees to speak their minds, it
   seemed there were some issues that some people were
   unwilling to share.

   How do you get people to open up? Create a sense
   of pride in the employees by asking them for their
   opinions when appropriate. By appropriate, we mean
   talking to you with genuine substance. For instance, if
   an employee wants to tell one of us that we're way off
   base about something, that's perfectly fine. Just don't

make baseless accusations. Have backup, evidence, and supporting information for what you're saying. It's important that they understand that, just like them, we're always looking to get better. But make sure they substantiate what they have to say.

4. **Communicate—Regularly and Through Proper Channels.** Another way to encourage employee communication is to make it a habit. Communicate with everyone in the company in a variety of ways on a regular basis, not just every now and then. For example, start holding weekly staff meetings. Initiate individual conversations with employees. Make it feel like the norm, not the exception.

   But remember you don't want to use that to eliminate the hierarchy in the company—you want your managers communicating as often and as comfortably as you do. So, if you're the owner and you've got layers of management, encourage people to speak frankly with their most immediate supervisor. For instance, if the forklift driver is having a problem and he bypasses his supervisor to talk with you, that can alienate the guy who's just been left out of the loop. You're overstepping the boundary of the hierarchy of the management system that you've put together. It also raises the question: why can't he go to his manager to talk? That can be a red flag that argues for a more comfortable communication environment at all levels of the company.

5. **Respond, Don't React.** A good leader looks for every opportunity to build trust and a sense of comfort with all employees. That's evident in our discussion regarding communication: if an employee is at ease talking

to a supervisor, owner, or anyone else, he's going to appreciate an environment that encourages that sort of candor.

Of course, you as the owner may hear things in those sorts of conversations that may not be the high point of your day. Some employees may merely complain, while others may point out something that they believe can be corrected. In either case, bear in mind an important rule of thumb: respond, don't react.

Here's what we mean by that. Let's say an employee, with the very best of intentions, comes to you and says a particular invoice is off by $5,000. That's a good chunk of change, and it can be awfully tempting to react: "What? Are you out of your mind? Where the hell did those numbers come from?"

If you react to that employee in that manner, it's a fair bet to say that he's likely going to be nervous about approaching you in the future—if, in fact, he approaches you at all.

Instead, choose to respond. For one thing, most employees share bad news out of a constructive concern for the well-being of the business—they want you to know something and to see if something can be done to correct it. And if that's the case, reacting out of emotion doesn't do anything to help address the issue.

So, take the time to respond. If an employee approaches you with news of a $5,000 disparity in an invoice, consider saying: "Wow. Can you walk me through how you came to that number?" Ask them to outline how they reached that particular conclusion. That kind of measured response not only moves the conversation toward a solution, but also lets the employee know that you value their input—both in letting you know about an issue as well as any steps that can be taken to correct the problem. That's leadership that fosters open, constructive communication.

6. **Work to Improve.** In an earlier chapter when we discussed the care and treatment of the idiots you'll inevitably encounter, we made the point of first making certain you're not the idiot. The same holds true with leadership. If there are any issues regarding employee trust, communication, and other important elements, first make certain you're not the problem.

   That means constantly working on your leadership skills and abilities. Ask yourself: Have any books come out on leadership that would be valuable for me to read? Have I considered coursework or continuing education to strengthen certain leadership skills? If you have a mentor, have you talked with him about ways to improve your leadership skills—and, if you don't have a trusted mentor, have you given any thought to developing such a relationship?

   Here it's essential that you critique yourself as aggressively as you might any other employee's performance. Don't be gun-shy about looking in the mirror and asking if your leadership is all it can be.

Being a great leader is a balancing act. On the one hand, that is your name on the door, and reputation is everything. But a great leader never exists in a vacuum—by consistently developing and displaying great leadership skills, you're doing everything possible to serve your employees to the best of your ability.

Moreover, being a great leader—and protecting that name on the door—also means having to make some very tough calls. For instance, in our company, we're constantly evaluating every employee, not just on current performance, but also on capacity to move up in the organization over time. And the tough reality is, not everyone who works for us is really geared to a long-term rise in position and responsibility. Like your horsemen, it's essential to recognize that point when your organization has outgrown an individual's capacity to contribute effectively. That means eventually making decisions that no one takes any pleasure in having to carry out.

But that's all part of being a great leader, both under the best of circumstances and the most challenging. Never lose sight that it's your name on the door. And great leadership is the most competitive advantage a company can have, regardless of what it's selling.

Chapter Ten

Whiteboarding

If you don't own a whiteboard, immediately make yourself a note to get one ASAP. This is an important take-away from this book.

We whiteboard everything. Brainstorming ideas, financial situations, legal situations, working through strategies, organizational charts, hub and spoke diagrams, new business ideas—basically any idea worth capturing on a whiteboard we put down. It is one of the simplest and most powerful habits we have established in our business.

If your memory is anything like ours, it's like a five gallon bucket with a hole in the bottom. The memory isn't very reliable and ideas don't stay for long. Great ideas pop into your head at some of the strangest times and they don't hang around very long. Whiteboarding will help you to capture them fast and concise or they will be lost in your brain's black hole where great ideas go to die.

We are very visual learners. When we lay ideas out in front of our eyes, it tends to click and imprint into our brains. It reminds us what to focus on. We get caught up in our everyday business and we lose sight of the things we need to do to innovate our business. On the flip side, we need to focus on the day-to-day business, so whiteboarding is also an unloading of our mental RAM. When you can unload on a whiteboard, it lessens the stress and you are able to think more clearly at the task on hand because everyone is focusing on the whiteboard.

As we mentioned earlier whiteboarding is simple, but we have been doing it for a long time, so it has become an easy exercise. For those of you who have never whiteboarded before, here are a few steps to get you started. Also remember that you can create your own steps or add to ours; this is your creative time.

- Explain the idea/topic: write down the big stuff.

- Never use the eraser: important.

- Encourage the ideas and expand: use different colored markers to make points.

- Organize information; provide more details on the big stuff.

- Think outside the box: be non-linear; get weird. This step is what I call reverse thinking. Think about what everyone would do with the idea, then do the opposite.

- Figure out why the idea won't work. This is the fun part: you get to be an asshole.

- Be specific on others' ideas; critique and record.

- Take a picture: this is maybe the most important step. You will go back and review whiteboarding sessions and they will remind you of your growth as a person and company.

Figure 1 is an example of a whiteboarding session that we did a few years ago. This particular session was about value and how we were going to deliver it to our customers. As you can see by the details, it was a very successful whiteboarding session.

The session in Figure 2 is interesting because it was our initial whiteboarding session regarding this book. As you can see it was a rough draft and it provided a great start for us. Also in the picture, you can see in the bottom left corner another whiteboarding session about a particular legal situation we were involved in that we covered in this book in an earlier chapter.

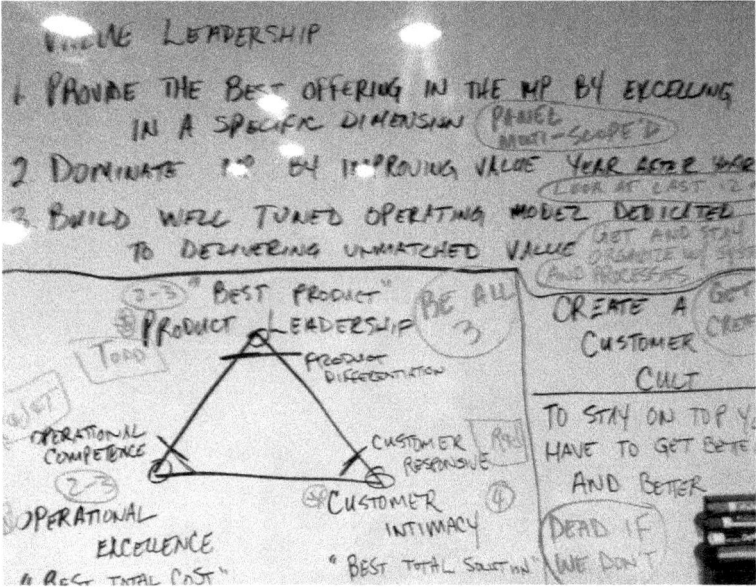

Figure 1

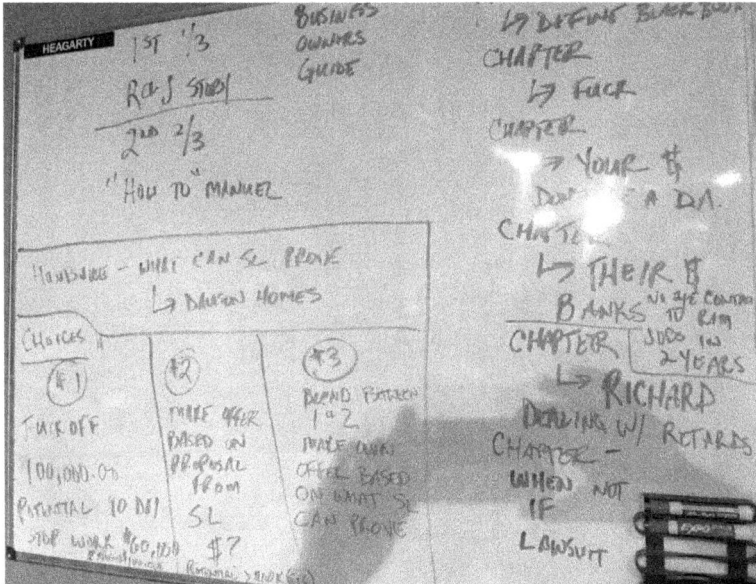

Figure 2

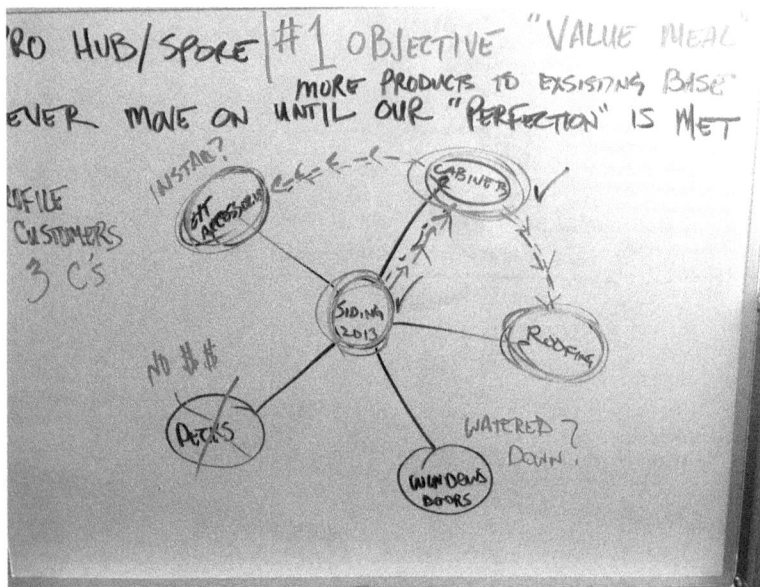

Figure 3

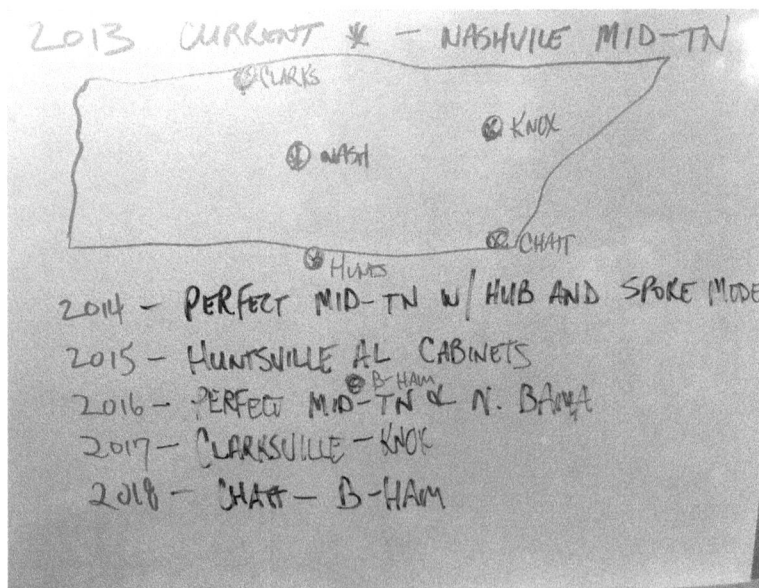

Figure 4

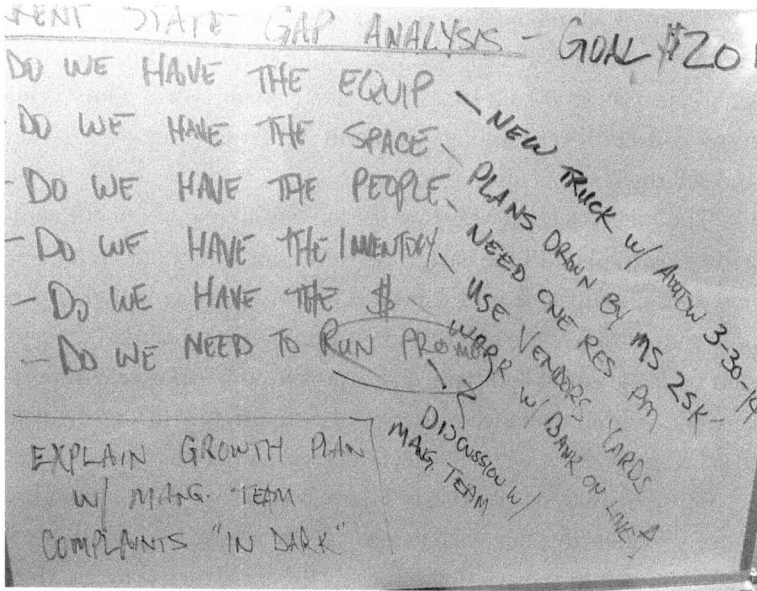

Figure 5

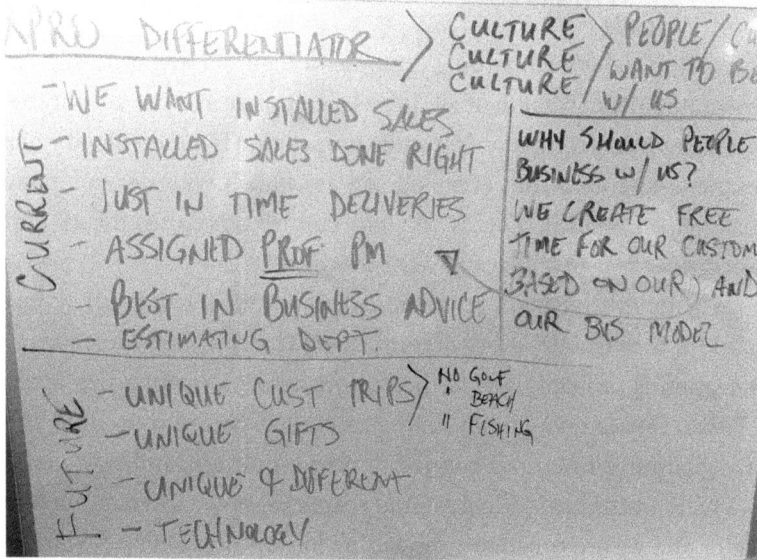

Figure 6

Figure 3 whiteboarding session was about our product growth and our "value meal" concept. Our "value meal" concept is exactly what the fast food industry has banked on for years. Our "value meal" concept is very similar: we bundle all of our products together and sell them at one all-in price.

The Figure 4 whiteboarding session was in regards to our company growth plan. In the early days we would survey our employees and their number-one complaint was that our Xpro growth plan was only shared inside the ownership group. We whiteboarded the session with the entire company and it proved to be an excellent exercise. We realized that once we had total company buy-in we were able to achieve our goals faster. Again, total transparency or open kimono.

The gap analysis exercise in Figure 5 is always the toughest because you identify your weaknesses as a company. It is hard to realize that you don't have the money or the inventory to grow. Most companies will not do this exercise and therefore their growth is stagnant or non-existent. You need to know your weaknesses, explore them, and correct them to properly grow both personally and professionally.

This final whiteboarding example in Figure 6 was probably the most important session of all. It was a complete exercise on our differentiator as a company. Our value proposition is our lifeblood—our engine—and each and every person associated with our company has helped build it. This is why our culture breeds teamwork and success. Our people like and want to win.

In today's business environment, innovation is incredibly important for virtually every organization. The constant quest for innovation is probably one of the reasons you are reading this book. We can't stress enough how important it is to record your ideas. We are guaranteed that our competition will innovate, and if we don't we will fall behind. Falling behind scares us, so we use it as a motivator and we are constantly discussing ideas around how we can get better every day.

Harmonic Alignment

To be a successful business owner, you have to be a solid leader. That's basically the crux of what we've been discussing throughout this book, touching on various elements, characteristics, and strategies that contribute to great leadership.

But gifted leadership doesn't always mean being at the front of the pack. It also involves living and working side by side with the various people who make up both your personal and professional life.

Every one of those people can either contribute to your success or detract from it. As the title of this chapter says, it's a question of overall harmonic alignment.

Aligning with Those Around You

Successful leadership involves a very simple formula. If you can maintain solid, positive relationships with those closest to you—your inner circle—then you're going to be successful. If you can't, you'll struggle, both in your business and elsewhere.

That begins with the people closest to you. You need to surround yourself with positive people, to feed off their energy and attitude. Of course, it's almost impossible to completely avoid negative people (remember, we had a chapter devoted to dealing with the idiots in your life!). But you need to filter out the negative and emphasize all that's positive. Put another way, you literally can will yourself to failure or you can will yourself to success.

We've talked extensively about the relationships you maintain with the professionals around you—your employees, partners, customers, and others. But they're not the only relationships that matter in your professional life. To truly succeed, you also need to be aligned with family members—spouses, children, as well as close friends.

It affects more than you might think. If you're unaligned in any aspect of your life, it affects you everywhere else. It's pervasive and very powerful. Lastly, if you are out of alignment in some manner, give yourself enough time to regain a sense of balance. Don't be impatient. Some forms of misalignment simply take longer to correct.

Rick's Story: Everybody Has a Part to Play

Recently, we had a long family discussion at the dinner table having to do with one of my kid's grades at school. It was far from a full crisis-mode conversation, but rather a sort of wake-up call—a chat that ultimately circled around to how everyone in our family has responsibilities that affect all of us.

For instance, our children are responsible for their performance in school. If they do well, then that's less we have to worry about as we prepare for college. Then we talked about what happens if my wife doesn't do her part. There's no dinner made, people aren't picked up and dropped off at certain times, and bills go unpaid. The entire household is utterly out of sync. Then we talked about me and my business, how if I don't do well at my job, there's no food on the table, no roof over our heads, and no money for college or other significant goals.

The point of the conversation wasn't meant to be overly negative—one misstep and everything comes crashing down!—but rather that everyone needs to be in alignment with everyone else. All of our responsibilities are complementary and, if one person doesn't hold up his or her particular responsibility, then everyone feels it. We're out of sync and everyone knows it.

I also know that I've been the most successful in my life when

I've been fully aligned with my wife. There's absolutely no question about it. That's when we're on the same page, not only about my business but with our children, our finances, everything.

That said, think about the relationship you have with your spouse or partner. When you're aligned, does everything in your life seem to be clicking? By the same token, when you're out of alignment in some way, does everything suffer as a result?

That carries over to everyone else in your life. Once you realize everyone is unique, you can build a strategy that aligns you with that person, whether it's your spouse, your business partner, children, or friends. That's where real success begins.

Are You Aligned?

That begs the question: how can you identify a strategy that will put you in alignment with those around you?

Again, that's specific to the person. For instance, with employees, alignment may be simply a matter of building their confidence in you, your business, and their place in it. With children, it's obviously a matter of affection, but also encouraging their understanding of their role in the family and, in turn, how that can impact every dynamic within the family.

So far as a spouse or partner is concerned, a few basic questions can help with ensuring a healthy alignment. Simply put: Does your spouse help you grow as a person? Are you making each other better through the years you spend together? Do you genuinely trust them and has that trust proved supportive in all aspects of your life?

If the answer to those questions is yes, then you're in alignment. And that will become evident in every aspect of your life. Moreover, whatever it is that you're doing to keep in alignment, stay the course. It's obviously working and the results are evident.

But don't take that for granted. Work at maintaining the alignment. With a spouse or partner, take the time every day to tell them how much they mean to you. With children, let them know how proud you are of all that they do. Alignment is an essential component of success, but one that needs ongoing attention and effort.

Watch for Misalignment

However much we want to remain consistently aligned with everyone in our lives, that's rarely possible. Often, negativity is all around you, and it's important to filter that as extensively as you can. As we've mentioned, if an employee is consistently negative or out of alignment with our business and the positive mindset we always strive to maintain, chances are good we'll eventually be forced to let that person go. It's by no means pleasant but absolutely necessary nonetheless.

Of course, that option isn't available when it comes to family members. For instance, in many families we know there's one or more members who are just wracked with envy. Maybe they're envious of someone else's personal success or jealous of the fact that they lack the strong relationships that some other family members enjoy. Whatever the reason, the envy is there for everyone to see. And, even more important, it impacts everyone, from a parent trying to run a business to a pre-teen trying to do his best in school.

In those cases, it's essential to strike a balance, one that distinguishes annoying behavior from the out-and-out destructive. For instance, let's say a family member is envious of your success and does little more than bitch about it on occasion. That's not particularly fun to be around, but it's not necessarily destructive to your personal or professional life. It's noise and little more than that.

By contrast, if someone in your family or circle of close friends seems aggressively negative when it comes to your personal or professional life—maybe they're talking behind your back or doing something else to try to deflate your success—take some advice we offered in an earlier chapter: look for common ground. Rather than cutting ties completely—which, in many cases, simply isn't possible—try to find some means of connecting with the other person within a positive framework. Look to establish some basis for a positive relationship. It may be sports or movies or whatever. But try to find something uplifting that, at the very least, works to offset pervasive negativity.

From there, filter out the negative as much as possible. Focus on whatever positive elements are present in the relationship. With a friend, if that simply isn't enough to help balance a lopsided sense of negativity, it may be appropriate to end the relationship or, at the very least, bring it down a few notches. Again, not a great deal of fun, but it may prove essential to both your personal and professional well-being.

Of course, cutting ties may not always be an option with a family member. In those instances, filter, then filter some more. Look to extract whatever benefits you can get from the relationship. Moreover, make sure whatever negativity exists impacts as little of your life—both personally and professionally—as much as possible. Try not to take the bait and instead focus on other matters that are of far greater benefit.

The Art of Compromise

Much of what we've been discussing in this chapter boils down to how you manage the relationships with those closest to you—and how those relationships impact the whole of your life. That may seem like a management issue—you do this and you get this sort of result—but, with personal matters, things are often not quite so cut and dried.

Take your relationships with family members. In that sphere, arguments are an inevitable part of life. Someone says they're not going to do something, so you respond accordingly. Voices are raised and sooner or later, an argument is in full swing.

As we said, that's just a part of life. But arguments don't have to be as destructive as they often can be. For instance, when things begin to escalate, look once more for common ground. Revisit what's been said and try to pinpoint stages where things become disconnected. Treat every individual from a singular perspective. If you think it might be beneficial, suggest forms of compromise that can defuse the situation.

Above all, ask yourself a critical question: would you rather be right or happy? When it comes to your business and its synergy with close family and friends, a happy alignment is always the better choice. Harmony in every aspect of your life, regardless of how you get there, is the key to success in whatever you do. Look for every opportunity to build and nurture it. It matters much more than you might think.

Chapter Twelve

Take a Sauna

S o, you're nearing the end of this book. We're confident that we've offered you some valuable guidance, not only with regard to your business but also how it relates to most every other aspect of your life.

Now, we'd like to pose a challenge to you: go take a sauna.

That probably seems like an odd request—particularly if you don't own or have access to a sauna—but it actually refers to a powerful call to action. In so many words, we hope you've learned a great deal from this book. Now is the time to put those ideas into action.

And it starts with taking a sauna.

Really.

Don't Just Do Something—Sit There

As you may have guessed, we have a sauna. In fact, we had it installed right in our company headquarters.

Obviously, we both really enjoy the physical relaxation that a sauna can offer. But, perhaps more important, what we really value is the environment it provides.

That's because it affords us complete solitude and privacy. For forty-five minutes or more, we know for a fact that it's just the two of us and the opportunity to share our thoughts and ideas. It's where our creativity can really flow. Our frame of mind totally shifts. We relax. It's genuinely amazing the sort of creative ideas and solutions we can come up with.

That's what we mean by urging you to go take a sauna. In reality, it can be a workout, a long walk, a round of golf, or most anything. It's about getting away from things, clearing your mind and getting a thirty-thousand-foot view of what you need to consider about your business and yourself. It's a time for pure thought with no distractions. Consider it your personal think tank.

Jay's Story: Sauna Equals Misery

Prior to meeting Rick my sauna time was extensive—and that was a good thing. A sauna brought me back to my high school and college wrestling days and the need to sit in a sauna and sweat endlessly until I made weight. It was a miserable experience.

But now I actually look forward to a sauna. As we explained, it's an opportunity for uninterrupted, focused thought. And if we have a specific problem to solve, chances are good someone's going to come up with an answer.

So, it's important to find your own sauna, whether that's a sauna itself or any other place that gives you a chance to step back and think about your business, yourself, your family, or whatever matters to you at the time.

Why a Sauna Matters

It's not hard to see the importance of a sauna. It's a tool that lets you move away from the day-to-day, hour-to-hour focus of running a business and instead think about the bigger picture. As the saying goes, you're not working *in* your business but *on* your business.

So why raise the issue now?

For one thing, we've been able to share some important ideas, concepts, and strategies with you—valuable stuff that you can begin using today to make both your life and business more successful.

But the rub is, you have to put those ideas into action.

Show of hands, please: how many of us have read a terrific book on a particular topic, put the book away, and, for one reason or another, never put any of that great advice into use? We thought so—a lot of people, and that includes us as well.

That's why this chapter is both a call to action and a call to step away and think about what you've learned. That way, you can put together a plan that makes the most of those ideas and concepts that you believe are best suited to your business. It may seem contradictory, but taking the time for a sauna—and doing so on a regular basis—means quiet time that can lead to the best form of action possible.

What to Do Next

Taking a sauna is a very personal, singular task, one that's geared to your business. That's why the idea behind a sauna is absolutely essential to know exactly what you're going to do next.

That said, however, here's one suggested way to go about that, a schematic of sorts that may prove helpful in taking powerful ideas and leveraging them to the max:

1. **Build a dashboard.** This means setting up a schedule of items to do as well as a means of tracking them. Be as detailed as you think you need to be. Include whatever you identify as critical to moving toward your ultimate goals.

2. **Identify a Clear Leader.** This is the guy where the buck stops, the final decision maker. Clarifying this from the outset sets up a hierarchy with which decisions are made efficiently and placed into action.

3. **Identify Resources.** What tools, assets, and other resources are available to you to meet your goals? This can include financial resources, personnel, and other items. Pinpointing these makes it clear in your mind as to those things you can rely on, time and again.

4. **Identify Obstacles.** What stands in the way of your success? It may be a particular competitor, the market as a whole, money, or some other problem. Know what you're up against. Prioritize them so you know which ones are the primary barriers to your overall objectives.

5. **Set up a timeline.** This takes in a number of time-related issues. First, set up a schedule to have certain important tasks completed. Again, that will vary from one business to the next—it may be financing for one, while another business may have to hire key personnel. Let your team know at the beginning of the week those goals that need to be reached over the next several days. Be crystal clear about your objectives. Don't just say: "Obtain financing." How much and under what terms? With whom and why? The more specific your goals, the better you're going to achieve precisely what needs to be done. If the overall list seems overwhelming, take things in smaller chunks. That can make important steps much more manageable.

6. **Set a regular schedule to monitor progress.** Plan to meet on a regular basis—say, weekly—to review progress. Encourage input from all team members to identify what went well and what still requires some adjustments.

7. **Set up comparatives.** One effective way to gauge over-all growth and progress is to measure them against other yardsticks. For instance, let's say we grew 25 percent last year. That sounds wonderful—and it is—but put that up against the overall market, which may have been up 13 percent. In effect, that means we really grew some 12 percent—a much more meaningful bit of information than stand-alone statistics. What you're looking for is "real" growth.

8. **Be ready to make adjustments.** No plan or course of action should be considered untouchable. By review-ing your progress on a regular basis and keeping open lines of communication, you'll know when things need to be corrected—or, by the same token, when some-thing is working really well and it's time to really hit the accelerator to fully leverage the opportunity.

You're most likely familiar with many of these ideas and sugges-tions.

Needless to say, feel free to pick and choose those that fit your particular circumstances. The overriding message is to have an empirical methodology in place, one that comes from the valuable sauna time you set aside to slow down and think. That way, you avoid the problem that many otherwise promising businesses stum-ble over: the tendency to fire, aim, and think. Instead, take the time to think, plan, and then do.

A Roadmap for the Rugged Roads

Obviously, every plan for the future is aimed at success. After all, why bother to plan in the first place for anything short of that?

But planning—and all that sauna time that suggests—is every

bit as valuable in another capacity. That's when you start hitting some hard times.

Believe us, no business on this planet is immune to challenging times. We've certainly been through them. And the time you spent mapping out plans and thinking carefully about where you're going and how become indispensable.

Let's be frank. Business is easy when things are good. Problems and headaches can be pushed to one side easily. People are easier to manage. It almost seems as though the business could function by itself, like a plane on autopilot sailing through clear blue skies.

But what happens when times get tough? You remember your purpose. You remember that you can't do everything yourself. You trust your people, you get out of the way, and you let them do what you trained them to do. You trust them. You think back on the lessons you've learned and the thinking, planning, and execution that got you to where you are now.

That circles back to your sauna time. That's when you set the concerns of the moment aside to consider those issues that are just now coming to the surface. How do I push my people but not too much? What about my personal leadership skills? When conditions become difficult, what can I do to make certain that my people retain their confidence in me and are willing to follow my lead and example? What can I do to inspire them?

Here, too, is where you'll come to appreciate the difference between motivation and inspiration. In a sense, motivation can come as a result of different forces. In some cases, you need someone else to motivate you. We've all been in that position and it works. The trouble is, it raises the question: if there hadn't been someone else, would you have been able to motivate yourself?

That's why a leader's overriding goal is to inspire. Looked at one way, that's also motivation, but one that occurs naturally. It doesn't necessarily need a push from someone else because it's already there.

By inspiring someone, you're allowing their own internal motivation to develop and eventually emerge.

Again, sauna time is where you have the opportunity to identify what truly inspires those around you and prompts them to follow you. When times are challenging, that's hardly the most opportune moment to sit back and ponder the meaning of inspiration and great leadership. If you've set aside sauna time, that's already in place.

Whatever You Do, Aim at the Bull's-eye

A discussion of what to do when times become challenging might suggest the value of setting modest goals. In a way, that's reasonable. When you're mapping out plans, it never makes sense to pursue the outrageous or outlandish. That's just a formula for frustration.

But that's not to suggest being overly reasonable or timid in your planning and thinking. Don't be shy about stretching things out and aiming for the bona fide bull's-eye. You may fall a little bit short, but you're still going to be way ahead of others who settle for "realistic" goals.

Moreover, it may sound corny, but don't limit your goals to just the financial. Don't misunderstand. Financial reward is great, but there's more to being truly successful than a fat bank account.

That's also part of sauna time. Use that opportunity to define what success really means to you in all its forms. For us, we've been fortunate enough to be able to change people's lives, whether they work for us, with us, or in some other capacity. Believe us, impacting someone's life means much more to us than any pot of gold. And that's the stuff that carries over, making you successful in every area of your life—in your business, your family, with your friends, and in your community.

Someone once said: "If you don't chase your own dreams, a guy like me will hire you to help me chase mine." Since you've read this book, it's certain you're the one chasing the dream. That's the challenge we want to leave you with. Take your sauna, decide what success means, and go after it. You won't be disappointed. Do something epic!

www.ingramcontent.com/pod-product-compliance
Lightning Source LLC
Chambersburg PA
CBHW071453200326

41519CB00019B/5724